Little Mammals of the Pacific Northwest

NORTHERN
FLYING SQUIRREL
(*Glaucomys sabrinus*)

Little Mammals of the Pacific Northwest

By ELLEN B. KRITZMAN

Pacific Search Press/nature

Cover and Book Design by Marilyn Weber

Cover Photo: Douglas squirrel *(Tamiasciurus douglasi)*

Published in the United States of America
by Pacific Search Press,
715 Harrison Street, Seattle, Washington,
and in Canada by J. J. Douglas Ltd.

Copyright © 1977 by Pacific Search
ISBN 0-914718-18-5
Library of Congress Catalog Card Number 76-58249
Manufactured in the United States of America

Contents

COLOR PHOTOS BY:

Jim and Elaine Butler: dusky shrew (pl. 3), heather vole (pl. 5), least chipmunk (pl. 8), marsh shrew (pl. 2), Pacific jumping mouse (pl. 2), shrew-mole (pl. 1), Townsend ground squirrel (pl. 6), water shrew (pl. 4)

John MacGregor: deer mouse (pl. 1), Gapper red-backed mouse (pl. 1), meadow vole (pl. 2)

Bernard Nist: Douglas squirrel (cover)

Thomas P. O'Farrell, Battelle-Northwest Photography: black-tailed jackrabbit (pl. 7)

Dennis R. Paulson: white-tailed antelope squirrel (pl. 8)

Grant Sharpe: Cascade golden-mantled ground squirrel (pl. 5), Columbian ground squirrel (pl. 5)

Joy Spurr: Olympic marmot (pl. 4)

John W. Thompson: muskrat (pl. 3), white-tailed jackrabbit (pl. 6)

BLACK AND WHITE PHOTOS BY:

Battelle-Northwest Photography: bushy-tailed wood rat (pp. 110-1), creeping vole (p. 56), Great Basin pocket mouse (p. 97), montane vole (p. 54), northern grasshopper mouse (p. 102), northern pocket gopher (p. 74), western harvest mouse (p. 45)

J. S. Dixon/INTERIOR-U.S. Fish and Wildlife Service: yellow-bellied marmot (p. 107)

Luther C. Goldman/INTERIOR-U.S. Fish and Wildlife Service: California ground squirrel (p. 44)

Linda Johnson: red squirrel (p. 63)

A. W. Moore/INTERIOR-U.S. Fish and Wildlife Service: mountain beaver (p. 35)

Bernard Nist: golden-mantled ground squirrel (p. 84), yellow-pine chipmunk (p. 81)

Charles J. Ott: pika (p. 67)

Dennis R. Paulson: sagebrush vole (p. 102), Washington ground squirrel (pp. 90-1)

Leonard Lee Rue III: beavers (pp. 51, 52)

Leonard Lee Rue IV: western gray squirrel (p. 39)

Victor B. Scheffer/INTERIOR-U.S. Fish and Wildlife Service: coast mole (p. 43)

Ward M. Sharp/INTERIOR-U.S. Fish and Wildlife Service: porcupine (p. 84)

Lloyd Smith: Heermann kangaroo rat (p. 101)

Joy Spurr: house mouse (p. 19)

Fred L. Tobiason: Townsend chipmunk (p. 25)

Washington State Game Department: northern flying squirrel (frontispiece), Nuttall cottontail (p. 106), snowshoe hare (p. 33)

O. J. White/INTERIOR-U.S. Fish and Wildlife Service: pygmy rabbit (p. 95)

Michael Wotton: red tree mouse (p. 28)

I am grateful to the many individuals who helped bring this book to completion, especially those who generously answered my plea for photographs of small mammals. In particular I would like to acknowledge the assistance of two persons. Dr. Murray Johnson, Curator of Mammals at the Puget Sound Museum of Natural History, helped in the search for illustrations and also reviewed and constructively criticized the entire manuscript. Jeanne Collins supported me in this literary effort from its inception and contributed greatly to the construction of the distribution maps. Thanks are also due to Lynn Erckmann, Research Technologist, Department of Zoology, University of Washington, for reviewing the botanical portions of the manuscript.

METRIC ABBREVIATIONS

The units of measurement from the metric system used in this book are as follows:

cm	centimeter
g	gram
ha	hectare
kg	kilogram
l	liter
m	meter
mm	millimeter

Additional abbreviation used:

C	centigrade

INTRODUCTION

Insectivores, Lagomorphs, and Rodents

The "little mammals" to which the title alludes belong to three groups which are classified as separate orders: insectivores (shrews and moles), lagomorphs (pikas, rabbits, and hares), and rodents (squirrels, rats, mice, and their relatives). In terms of average size they are certainly on the small side. Individual species, however, range from the tiny flyweight shrew of one-quarter ounce (7 to 8 g) or so to the welterweight beaver, which at forty pounds (18 kg) and more is hardly a diminutive animal.

The insectivores are a group of ancient origin, and some

long-ago types were probably ancestral to all other placental mammals. Insectivores still retain a small brain that is not highly evolved. The skeleton of the shrew has maintained essentially the same generalized form as the primitive mammal, including five-toed feet placed flat on the ground. The shape is mouselike, but with a long, narrow snout. The tail is generally scaly but covered with short hairs. The fur is soft and dense, the eyes and ears small. As a group the shrews are the smallest of all mammals. According to physiological rules, the smaller a warm-blooded animal the higher its metabolic rate must be. The tiniest shrews are close to the limit in size beyond which they would need an infinite amount of oxygen and could never get enough to eat. They usually require two-thirds or more of their own weight in food each twenty-four hours, which necessitates almost continuous activity with only intermittent periods of rest. Their diet consists of various insects, worms, and small vertebrates. They have very high-pitched voices, and there is now some evidence that they may use echolocation in their hunting, after the manner of bats.

Moles are in several ways similar to shrews—the primitive brain, the dentition, and the long snout, for instance—but have undergone great specialization for a burrowing or fossorial mode of life. Their forearms are short and wide with heavy muscles; their forefeet are broad, strongly clawed, and permanently turned outward—all adaptations for digging. In fact, their physique might be the envy of the male of the species *Homo sapiens:* while the shoulders are wide and strongly muscled, the hips are very narrow, enabling the steam-shovel front end of the mole to pass the hind end as it turns in its tunnel. The thick, velvety fur is not disturbed by movement in either direction. The long snout and short tail are sensitive appendages, but the minute eyes function at a minimal level and external ears are absent. The mole probably "hears" sound waves with its whole body—so keenly, it is able to detect the vibrations of a worm digging. Like shrews, moles have voracious appetites, with a particular taste for earthworms. These constitute 75 percent to 80 percent of their diet; the other 25 percent or so is plant food.

The rabbits and their relatives used to be lumped with the rodents by both scientists and laymen. Members of the two orders do have similar diets and therefore similar adaptations for eating. A pair of enlarged incisors designed for gnawing are separated by a long gap from the back grinding teeth. On closer examination, however, the teeth of the two groups show quite a different pattern, the lagomorphs sporting a small additional pair of upper incisors behind the large pair. In fact, lagomorphs and rodents have followed separate evolutionary lines since the time of their earliest fossil records in the long-ago Paleocene.

All of the lagomorphs have short or nonexistent tails, but only the rabbits and hares are adapted as hopping forms with very long, strong hind limbs, and with extremely elongated ears for acute hearing. The true hares, some of which are known as jackrabbits, have the most highly developed ears and hind legs. They also bear young that are called "precocial," meaning they are fully developed at birth and very soon able to follow mother and fend for themselves. In contrast, the "altricial" young of the rabbits are born blind, naked, and helpless.

Rodents are incredibly numerous in individual numbers as well as in kind and probably have been since the start of the Cenozoic era some 70 million years ago. According to Harvey Gunderson (*Mammalogy*, 1976), there are about 1,684 species of rodents and only approximately 2,289 of all other mammal species combined. The rodent order includes not only a great diversity of species of rats and mice but also squirrels, chipmunks, pocket gophers, beavers, porcupines and muskrats. Their success can be attributed at least in part to their rapid rate of reproduction, their adaptation to numerous environments (all except open sea or air), and their generally small size. I qualified the last phrase because there are, and have been, some notable exceptions. The modern beaver is the largest rodent living in North America; a scant million years ago there were giant beavers the size of small bears.

Rodents have always been primarily herbivorous and characteristically equipped with an upper and a lower pair of large chisellike incisors. During the life of the animal these teeth are continually growing and being sharpened as one pair works against the other while at the same time gnawing and digging wear them down. The plant food, once gnawed off, must be ground by the back teeth, so the lower jaw is hinged to the skull in a manner that permits its movement back and forth, up and down, and sideways. The skull is quite long and low, accommodating a brain developed not much beyond that of the insectivore. The rest of the skeleton is not highly specialized in most rodents. The limbs are fairly flexible, permitting a variety of movements. Through evolution one toe may be lost on the front feet, or all five retained back and front. The feet are placed flat, or nearly flat, on the ground.

A number of rodents ride out periods of inclement weather and food shortages by going into a dormant state. A winter dormant period is called hibernation, a summer one aestivation, but the physiology of the two appears to be the same. Body temperature falls to within a degree or two of the den or burrow temperature, metabolism and oxygen consumption are greatly reduced, heartbeat and respiration drop sharply. In its dormancy the true hibernator usually lives on energy stored in the form of body fat. Other animals enter a torpid state in winter, but do not experience such a physiological shutdown, and awake periodically to utilize food caches rather than internal fat deposits. Most northwest chipmunk species fall into this category and are easily roused from their winter sleep, while a hibernator may take hours to warm up sufficiently to become active.

The largest family of Pacific Northwest rodents is the Cricetidae. The mice of this family are quite clearly separable into two types—so clearly that many authorities consider them different families, Cricetidae and Microtidae. The typical cricetid is the deer mouse type: pointed muzzle, relatively large eyes, large ears, and relatively long tail. The other is the vole or meadow mouse type: blunt muzzle, quite small eyes, small ears, and relatively short tail.

Why Small Mammals

Certainly I ought to take the positive view and assume there are no doubters or scoffers among you asking, "Why small mammals?" "Who's interested in such dirty pestiferous vermin as moles, rats, and mice?" However, you must excuse me if I feel compelled to devote at least a little space to extolling the worth of our native mammals of the smaller dimensions. All anthropomorphic adjectives are quite intentional. May they help make the small gnawers and burrowers as likable to the reader as they are to me.

I readily admit that I like shrews and mice and their kin for no other reason than that they exist. They are fascinating for their adaptations to a variety of life-styles—for gliding silently among the dense conifers in the darkness of the night, for burrowing deep in underground tunnels where blindness is no handicap, for swimming in cold, swift mountain streams in a waterproof coat, for maintaining life in the hottest, driest desert barrens. I admire their domesticity. Many are energetic creatures working long hours to construct lodges or tunnel systems, or at the very least shallow burrows equipped with cozy, warm ball- or cup-shaped nests. Not a few labor industriously to lay in supplies for the long winter months. If you have ever been beguiled while watching the antics of a chipmunk or squirrel, you would undoubtedly appreciate the delights of having a secret peephole for observing the daily activities of some of the other little mammals whose secluded or nocturnal worlds are usually closed to you.

I am likewise amazed every time I consider the fact that a creature as tiny as a shrew-mole is just as much a warm-blooded mammal as any human and has all the same bodily functions. Consider the tiny heart beating, the blood circulating, the little muscles contracting in coordinated movements, the breath going in and out of the infant shrew-mole. It would measure about an inch (25 mm) in length and weigh but a fraction of an ounce ($\frac{1}{2}$ g or so).

I cannot claim that all insectivores, lagomorphs, and rodents are handsome creatures, but many of our native ones are. Few have the drab colors and naked scaly tails of the black and Norway rats or the house mouse, that infamous trio that exemplifies rodents to so many people. Nor do I think our little native mammals are such unrelieved villains as these rat and mouse immigrants from the Old World. The only really redeeming feature of the latter has been their use as original breeding stock for strains of experimental laboratory animals.

To my mind there is more on the credit than the debit side of the ledger where our native forms are concerned. It is true that certain of them can carry diseases potentially dangerous to man, such as sylvatic plague, tularemia, and Rocky Mountain spotted fever. However, since the animals do not cohabit with man, the chance of any epidemic outbreak among the human population is extremely thin.

Where there are high populations locally, some species may become pests to farmers and gardeners owing to plants eaten or the detrimental effects of other activities. For example, forest plantations can be damaged by snowshoe hares, squirrels, porcupines, or deer mice. The last are particularly efficient destroyers of forest tree seed. Orchards are attacked by certain field mice and voles. Fields of grain and alfalfa are vulnerable, particularly to certain colonial rodents. The coast mole is not beloved of every gardener, orchardist, or golf course operator. A maze of gopher mounds in the middle of a pasture is good for neither cattle nor farm machinery. Yet there are beneficial effects stemming from the very same activities. The plants consumed may be noxious weeds; the insects eaten, species harmful to crops or livestock. Burrowing activities do aerate and cultivate the soil, helping it to retain moisture. As the basic food source for many predators, small wild mammals may help to remove predator pressure from livestock and other "desirable" animals. A few, like the rabbits and hares, are good edible game species. Others, like the beaver and muskrat, yield valuable furs and played an important part in the exploration and settlement of the West.

Using
This Book

There are big hardback volumes and little field guides in which you could seek descriptions and identifications of all the North American mammals. However, few are devoted to the Pacific Northwest or attempt to cover that region in detail. None devote themselves to the small gnawers and burrowers. More important, none group their descriptions of the animals by habitat, as they are found in nature. Instead, they are usually put into taxonomic units according to their evolutionary relationships. Maybe you will use this book sitting in your favorite armchair, planning a trip, or reminiscing over a past one.

Maybe you will actually carry it with you into the damp ferny depths of the coastal forest, the sun and sagebrush of the desert, the glacial cirques and flowery meadows of the high mountain terrain. By looking at the appropriate habitat section, you have readily available the major small mammals that seek bed and board there.

For the purposes of this book I have chosen to define the Pacific Northwest as Oregon, Washington, Idaho, and southern British Columbia. The animals naturally do not feel bound to honor state and provincial borders, but farther north a whole new complex of species tends to replace its southern counterpart. Also, the region defined does share a certain uniformity of habitat types. Twelve habitats, or associations of a particular climate, landform, and flora are described. Where an association relates to one or more life zones the latter are mentioned, since the life zone concept is a useful one familiar to so many with an interest in natural history. The biologist C. Hart Merriam proposed it at the end of the nineteenth century. He tied in the distribution of North American plants and animals with temperature, and described those temperature bands or zones that would be found at particular altitudes and latitudes across the continent. Other climatic variables, particularly precipitation, while secondary to temperature, do play important roles in establishing the character of the life zones. In the Pacific Northwest there are five life zones, ranging from the hot, dry desert or semidesert of the Upper Sonoran through the Transition, the Canadian, and the Hudsonian, to the chilly, windswept, and frequently snow-laden peaks of the Arctic-Alpine.

Following the description of each association, I have introduced those small mammals that make the area their primary habitat. Provided are their identifying characteristics, some comments on habits and biology, and a rough range map (based on distribution maps of Hall and Kelson, *The Mammals of North America*, 1959). At the end of each section is a list of other little mammals to be seen in that association. Refer to the index to locate the major discussion of each species.

For those species that have been slighted, I sincerely apologize—both to them and to the reader. There are simply too many small mammals to make a full discussion of each reasonable or desirable. Some, particularly those very rare in their occurrence or very restricted in their range, must content themselves with being mentioned under a generic relative of similar habits and habitat.

Nonnative species have been omitted. Some have become quite common, but usually within the confines of the areas in which they were originally released. One example is the eastern gray squirrel, *(Sciurus carolinensis)* of such cities as Seattle, Spokane, and Vancouver, British Columbia. Another is the nutria *(Myocastor coypus)*, a large brown rodent with a round scaly tail whose forefathers took up residence in local waterways after release by insolvent fur farmers. The eastern cottontail *(Sylvilagus floridanus)*, on the other hand, had several sites of introduction along the western coast as well as in eastern Washington. It flourished and spread in all those areas where there was growth of brush or mixed types of herbaceous vegetation and can be confused with the native Nuttall cottontail. The eastern is slightly larger and has a distinctly brown tone to the coat, whereas the Nuttall has more gray. The Old World rats *(Rattus rattus* and *R. norvegicus)* and the house mouse *(Mus musculus)* are admittedly both common and widespread. However, their sphere of activity is primarily man's buildings and stores, their habits only too well known to him. The house mouse has spread out widely from rural areas but, along with the rats of the same family, can quite easily be distinguished from similar native forms by its naked scaly tail and overall uniformity of color—no pretty white belly here.

There is one mouse that defies the ecologist to pin it down to one or even a few preferred habitats, making itself quite at home in all communities and at all elevations from sea level to above timberline. It even replaces the house mouse as resident pest in cabins and isolated structures. Thus the introduction seems the best place for the description of the deer mouse *(Peromyscus maniculatus,* pl. 1). It is quite a handsome mouse as mice go, with large ears, brown to gray fur (blue

HOUSE MOUSE (*Mus musculus*)

gray in the youngsters) on the upper parts and white on the underparts, this contrast extending the length of a moderately long tail.
There are innumerable subspecies differing slightly in coloration and
tail length, but the general range of dimensions is 3½ to 4 inches (89 to
102 mm) for head and body, 2½ to 4 inches (64 to 102 mm) for tail.

     The deer mouse remains active throughout the year and one
often sees its tiny tracks in the fresh snow. Never unsociable where its
fellows are concerned, the deer mouse may sleep in a heap of other
mice in winter to conserve warmth. The deer mouse appears bright
and engaging, and always ready to take advantage of what opportu-
nity offers. Thus, its small cup-shaped nest may be found in a variety of
places: in a hollow log, under a rock, in a shallow burrow dug by itself
or appropriated from another animal, even in some of the bizarre spots
recorded by one naturalist—an unused typewriter, the pocket of an
old coat, the mummified but still-furry remains of a dead wood rat. I
have turned over old boards and found deer mouse nests incorporat-

ing Kleenex and other man-made materials, but never a prettier nest than I was privileged to see recently. I have rescued untold numbers of animals, cold-blooded as well as warm-blooded, from cats. Many were beyond help; most of the others I released instantly. However, this particular little deer mouse, when finally dropped by the offending cat, lay on its back, apparently in shock, badly skinned in two places. I administered an eyedropper of wine and water, my standard antishock treatment, applied antibiotic ointment, and placed the mouse in a small cage with some water, raisins, and a piece of peanut-buttered carrot. I supplied two Kleenex. Within a few hours the tissues were partially shredded, very finely, and arranged in a lovely ring within which the mouse himself was tightly curled. I felt that his back might be bare from lack of materials rather than choice, and put in one more Kleenex. By the following morning the mouse had drawn it up over himself and was ensconced in a soft, white igloo. I only wished I had seen the work in progress. I might add that his nest remained white and unsullied. For his bathroom the mouse chose the opposite corner of the cage.

With respect to food, the deer mouse, though partial to seeds, takes whatever is in season locally: plant greens, mushrooms, lichens, adult and larval insects, other meat. Some food is stored away for severe winter weather dining. The female of the species is quite prolific, usually producing four or more litters of young a year. This offsets the toll taken by a number of carnivorous birds and mammals for whom the deer mouse is a dietary staple. The hours between sunset and sunrise form the usual period for the deer mouse to be active. All members of the species are good runners and skillful climbers, but the deer mouse of the mountain forests, considered by some a distinct species *(P. oreas),* has the longest tail and is the most accomplished at arboreal maneuvering.

ASSOCIATIONS

Coastal Forest

The coastal forest, lying within the Humid Transition Life Zone, is a dense, moist coniferous and deciduous forest. Precipitation there is usually quite heavy–30 to 100 inches (76 to 254 cm) or more a year. Winters are mild with little snowfall; summer temperatures are moderate and rarely reach ninety degrees Fahrenheit (32°C). This is a low-elevation forest, rarely extending upwards beyond approximately 3,000 feet (914 m). The most characteristic conifers present are Douglas fir, western hemlock, western red cedar, and Sitka spruce. Deciduous species include alder, dogwood, and maple. Mosses and ferns are common.

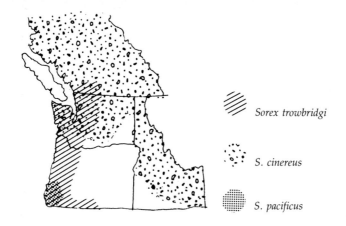

Sorex trowbridgi

S. cinereus

S. pacificus

Trowbridge shrew *(Sorex trowbridgi)*
A medium-sized shrew of about 4½ inches (114 mm) plus, the Trowbridge has a long tail which is distinctly bicolored. The body of this shrew is sooty or bluish gray above, slightly lighter underneath.

The Trowbridge shrew may be found living as high as timberline but is most common in the dense lowland coniferous forest. Here it lives out its appointed year and a half at a somewhat more leisurely pace than the smaller vagrant shrew *(S. vagrans)*. To the insectivore's usual diet of forest floor isopods, insects, and worms, the Trowbridge shrew adds quite a bit of plant food, including the seeds of the Douglas fir. The breeding season opens around April and one litter is usual, though other pregnancies have been known to follow the first in quick succession.

The masked or cinereous shrew *(S. cinereus)* is a much rarer animal in the coastal forests, as well as in the mountain forests. Smaller than the Trowbridge, it measures close to four inches (102 mm) in length. It is brown to grayish above and a distinctly paler shade of the same beneath. When a litter is born, following a seventeen- to eighteen-day gestation period, there are anywhere from four to ten blind, hairless infants, each weighing about 0.1 gram (less than 0.01 oz). Twenty days later they are almost adult size and independent.

The Pacific shrew *(S. pacificus)* is one of the larger *Sorex,* about six inches (152 m) in length. It is very clearly a brown shrew, including its tail, with the belly only slightly lighter in color. It seeks out the damp habitat of decaying logs and wet brush in the coastal spruce and redwood forests of western Oregon.

Townsend chipmunk *(Eutamias townsendi)*
The Townsend, a large chipmunk of ten inches (254 mm) or more,

TOWNSEND CHIPMUNK *(Eutamias townsendi)*

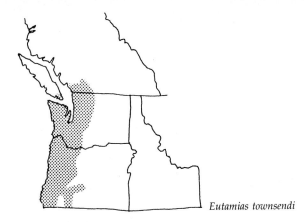

Eutamias townsendi

tends to have a dark coat with dull stripes. The underside of its tail is reddish brown with marginal hairs that are partially white.

The Townsend chipmunk is found in brushy areas and at the edges of clearings in the denser forests of the Humid Transition and Canadian life zones. It is an agile climber, but less active and of a less nervous temperament than the yellow-pine chipmunk *(E. amoenus)*. Though diurnal, the Townsend is less often seen than heard giving its shrill "chip" call. It must believe in the adage that variety is the spice of life, for its diet includes seeds, nuts, berries, roots and bulbs, flowers, fungi, insects, and so forth. Nuts and seeds are buried in caches, and some of these stores are used periodically throughout the winter while the animal remains underground. The young are born in May, appear above ground in June, and are nearly full-grown and on their own by August. These young-of-the-year gather and store their own food for the coming winter, and make their own nests, lining them with dry grass—as they will do for each of the five years or so that constitute their natural life-span in the wild.

Gapper red-backed mouse,
boreal red-backed vole *(Clethrionomys gapperi)*
The red-backed mice all look like typical voles (blunt-nosed, small-eared, and short-tailed mice), but can be recognized by the definitely reddish band on the back. The Gapper red-back (pl. 1) is about six inches (152 mm) long with buffy gray sides and a light belly.

The Gapper red-back is a mouse of the dense coniferous forests, irrespective of elevation, although in the higher mountains it may also be found in more open meadow and riparian habitats and in rockslide areas. It is found frequently associated with rotten logs or tree roots. Yet it is not so dependent on plant cover protection as meadow

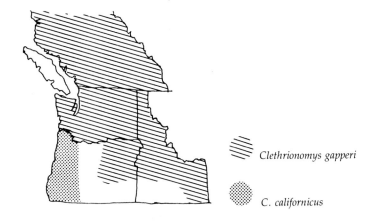

Clethrionomys gapperi

C. californicus

mice and leaves the construction of runways to the latter. The Gapper red-backed mouse is active day and night through all seasons, tunneling through the snow in winter. It climbs well but nests underground beneath logs or litter.

Recent research has shown that fungi make up a great portion of the diet of *Clethrionomys,* though it also eats seeds, bark (occasionally girdling trees), insects, and green plant material. Its presence may be advertised by pieces of cut grass and plants drawn under the cover of logs to be eaten in unhurried safety. The Gapper red-backed mouse has two or more litters a year, each with about four young. Though usually neither abundant nor regular in its distribution, its population may at times rival that of the deer mouse locally.

The western or California red-backed mouse *(C. californicus)* is the counterpart of the Gapper in the damp, dark coniferous forests of the coast south of the Columbia River. It is a little bit larger, darker, and duller in its red banding. This vole dwells in western Oregon in the Humid Transition Life Zone or in the Canadian Zone of the coastal mountains. Like the Gapper in habits, the California red-backed mouse is even more closely tied to decaying log habitats, probably because of their fungal growth.

Red tree mouse *(Arborimus longicaudus)*

The red tree mouse is a pretty fellow, light rust color to cinnamon on the back, and below, white over gray underfur. Its tail is dark and very long for a vole (about 70 percent of its total length), to suit the need of an arboreal animal for a good balancing appendage.

Yes indeed, a mouse that lives in the trees—in fact, 100 feet (30 m) or more above the ground in fir, hemlock, and spruce! It travels from tree to tree, remaining high above the ground in the dense

27

RED TREE MOUSE *(Arborimus longicaudus)*

28

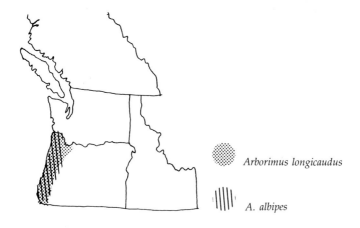

Arborimus longicaudus

A. albipes

coniferous forest. Needles provide its food, particularly those of the Douglas fir. Some needles may be eaten on the spot, but frequently entire terminal twigs are carried home to be worked on there. According to one observer, 100 needles an hour is an average rate of consumption. The red tree mouse is a good conservationist. The needle residue (vein and resin ducts) is then used to construct huge nests wedged into tree forks, set atop large branches, or even built around the trunks. These nests are said to contain up to a bushel of needle parts, twigs, and mouse droppings, hardened and compacted into a waterproof dome. They are really houses rather than nests, for each contains several nests connected by tunnels and is used by successive generations. The young of the red tree mouse are slow in their development, and for some time they can easily be dragged to safety by the mother. Though you will seldom see a tree mouse, it is not an uncommon animal within its range.

The dusky tree mouse *(Arborimus l. silvicola)* is now considered simply a subspecies of the red tree mouse. On the other hand, the white-footed tree mouse *(A. albipes)* is more of a ground dweller and thus more like the heather vole *(Phenacomys intermedius)*. The tail of the white-footed tree mouse is intermediate in length between those of the other two species. Like the red tree mouse, it is an inhabitant of dense forest, but is even rarer and less well known than the uncommon heather vole.

ALSO LOOK FOR: Vagrant shrew
　　　　　　　　Shrew-mole
　　　　　　　　Snowshoe hare
　　　　　　　　Northern flying squirrel
　　　　　　　　Douglas squirrel
　　　　　　　　Mountain beaver
　　　　　　　　Pacific jumping mouse

Moist Scrub and Thicket

In life zone position and general geographic location, the association of moist scrub and thicket is inseparable from that of the coastal forest. Therefore the two share the same climatic conditions. Often, in fact, moist scrub forms the tangled understory of the coastal forest. In other places it extends beyond the woods to cover hillsides and ravines. The plant components include ferns, salal and kinnikinnick, Oregon grape, devil's club, blackberry and salmonberry. The forest offers a floor of leaf litter and cones for some terrestrial species and the trees themselves for arboreal or gliding forms; the moist scrub offers the protective cover and forage of greens and woody shrubs which several other species prefer or require.

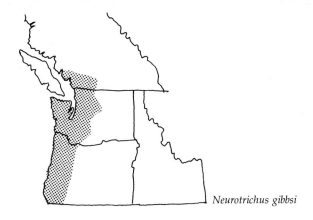

Neurotrichus gibbsi

Shrew-mole *(Neurotrichus gibbsi)*

As its name indicates, this little mammal is a mole that might well be mistaken for a shrew. The shrew-mole (pl. 1) measures only 4½ inches (114 mm). It has short, sooty or blackish gray fur and a short, fat, scaly tail clothed in bristly hairs. Its forefeet are broadened more than those of the shrews, but less than those of the larger moles. Thus it walks with greater agility than the latter, and also climbs and swims well. However, in burrowing it pushes the soil to each side after the manner of the larger moles as long as the soil is not too hard for such a miniature digger to handle.

The shrew-mole is partial to damp, shady ravines and dense, moist underbrush in the lowlands. Nevertheless, its range does extend up into the mountains, particularly in the vicinity of forest streams. It is not a rare animal, but its life history has been given little attention—more should be given. Once, in my enthusiastic graduate student days, I thought to remedy this situation myself. I captured a few in sunken tin cans, I provided them homes in aquariums filled with dampened peat moss, I fed them lavishly on dog food and mealworms (which they always grabbed avidly and carried underground immediately). I watched them explore and eat and tunnel. I monitored their extensive intervals of activity over the course of twenty-four-hour periods. But never did I feel I got to know the essence of their being, and grew disheartened because each little shrew-mole survived but a few months at most in captivity.

The shrew-mole is interesting not only for being an "in-between" animal, but for being unique to the Pacific Northwest; its closest relatives are Oriental species. Like the shrew, the shrew-mole forages day and night in subsurface runways under the leaf litter. It hunts down earthworms, insects, and spiders by probing with its

SNOWSHOE HARE *(Lepus americanus)*

sensitive nose and is said to be able to detect the vibrations of a worm digging, just as the larger moles can. A litter of four, usually born in April, may be raised in a leaf nest in a rotten log.

Snowshoe hare, varying hare *(Lepus americanus)*
The snowshoe is a hare of about sixteen inches (406 mm) intermediate in size between the larger jackrabbits and the smaller cottontails. It has relatively short ears for a hare, but much longer hind feet than the rabbits. Normally its coat is brown in summer and white in winter, but in the coastal lowlands where successive generations experience only minimal snowfalls, the varying hare declines to vary—it remains brown all year.

The snowshoe hare is partial to brushy undergrowth and streamside thickets but may be found in wooded areas at any eleva-

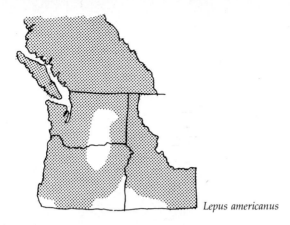

Lepus americanus

tion. It is usually sufficiently camouflaged to be inconspicuous and disappears quickly down its well-kept runways at the first sign of danger. The home range of one individual encompasses an area of ten to fifteen acres (4 to 6 ha).

The name *snowshoe* refers to the stiff, dense hairs on its hind feet which enable this hare to move easily over the soft snow. The deepening snow is no threat to the snowshoe hare's food supply; it simply raises the animal up to the level of fresh buds, twig tips, and bark. When hare populations are high, forest trees, fruit trees, and ornamentals may suffer. In summer, grasses and herbaceous vegetation are eaten instead. In turn, the snowshoe hare is a prime food source for several large predators, such as bobcat, Canada lynx, and fox, as well as hawks and owls.

Rabbits and hares are generally considered silent, but the snowshoe hare has quite a repertoire: a scream means injury or capture, a grunt or growl denotes anger or fear, a drumming or thumping of the hind feet alarms others or forms part of a March courtship "dance." In common with other hares, the snowshoe makes no real burrow or nest, just a shallow depression called a form, in which the precocial young are born after a thirty-six-day gestation period.

Mountain beaver *(Aplodontia rufa)*
You ought to know at the start that the mountain beaver is not principally a mountain form nor in any way related to the beaver. Rather, it is somewhat reminiscent of a muskrat that has lost its tail through misadventure. The mountain beaver is about fourteen inches (356 mm) long and has short blackish brown fur overlaid by longer, coarser guard hairs. It has fairly long claws and small beady black eyes which see but poorly.

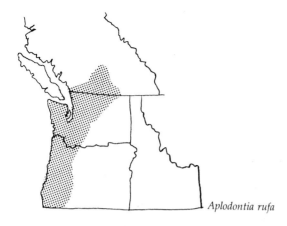

Aplodontia rufa

The mountain beaver seeks moist places: berry tangles and dense underbrush in the coastal forest, streamside thickets, the deciduous jungle of ravines. Most common in the Humid Transition Life Zone, it is also found at higher elevations up into the Hudsonian. Like the shrew-mole, it is an animal unique to the Pacific Northwest. Its anatomy, especially the skeletal parts, also set it apart as something rather special—the oldest living rodent species.

The mountain beaver is usually silent and generally shy, except during breeding season or when one thinks it is being molested. A strict vegetarian, it dines on most of the shrubs and plants of its habitat, including berry bushes, bracken fern, skunk cabbage, and even nettles and devil's club, inedible as these would seem. Entire plants are sometimes drawn into the burrow and a portion of them may be dried and stored in special chambers for winter use. The mountain

MOUNTAIN BEAVER *(Aplodontia rufa)*

beaver remains more or less active through the winter, moving about under the snow. In March or April two to four babies are born. They mature slowly, not reaching adulthood until their second year.

The mountain beaver home is a mazelike system of shallow tunnels, quite prone to collapse, with numerous openings (six inches or 152 mm in diameter) dug under brush, supporting tree roots, or logs. The mountain beaver may make itself an unwelcome nuisance by undercutting large areas with these burrows, as well as by debarking or otherwise damaging trees and shrubs. The Northwest Coast Indians turned it into a useful animal, however, by making its fur into robes and blankets.

ALSO LOOK FOR: Vagrant shrew
Trowbridge shrew
Pacific shrew
Coast mole
Townsend chipmunk
Creeping vole
Western and Pacific jumping mice

Oak Woods
and Chaparral

The word chaparral has been used loosely to mean any impenetrable thicket of a fairly dry area and in that sense could be applied to the scrub associated with the open pine forests of the interior. However, I have used chaparral in its more limited sense of comprising a particular association of shrubs best known in California, but spreading north into southwestern Oregon. It covers the drier and more exposed ground west of the Cascades, where precipitation does not exceed twenty inches (51 cm) a year. Component shrubs include species of the three genera: Ceanothus (including buckbrush and deer brush), Arctostaphylos (including manzanita), and Cercocarpus (the genus of mountain mahogany). Other plants, such as wild rose and bitter cherry, may be part of the association. The Garry or white oak grows in the same areas but also extends farther north beyond the range of chaparral. Madrona not infrequently grows alongside the Garry oak. A second species of oak, the live oak, gets no farther north than Oregon.

Sylvilagus bachmani

Brush rabbit *(Sylvilagus bachmani)*
The brush rabbit is a small, dark, brownish cottontail about twelve inches (305 mm) long, its tail not quite the pristine white powder puff of other *Sylvilagus* species.

The chaparral and thick brush of coastal Oregon provide prime habitat for this rabbit. Never venturing far from its thicket home, it feeds on grasses, clover, and the like, going only as far as the edges of open fields and pastures. The brush rabbit eats little woody food, since greens are usually available to it all year. Perhaps even shier than most rabbits, it is rarely abroad during the day except to bask in the very early sunshine. Then it relies on its concealing coloration and sits motionless in trails and roadways. Three or four litters are customarily produced by every pair of brush rabbits between January and June.

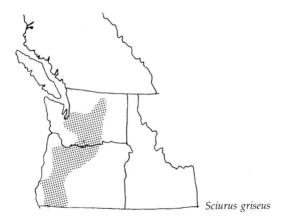

Sciurus griseus

WESTERN GRAY SQUIRREL *(Sciurus griseus)*

Western gray squirrel *(Sciurus griseus)*

Our native western gray squirrel is a handsome animal with a big bushy tail, its long fur silvery gray above and whitish below. It is a large and imposing squirrel, some twenty-two inches (559 mm) in length.

The western gray squirrel likes the drier, more open woods from central Washington south, and is usually associated with oak trees. Acorns are its staple food, though the seeds of Douglas fir, pines

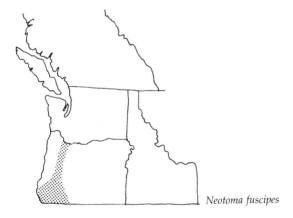

Neotoma fuscipes

39

(particularly yellow pine in the summer), and other trees are also eaten. The cambium layer of the tree trunks when the sap first rises also appeals to this squirrel's taste. Nuts and seeds are gathered each autumn and buried in holes a few inches deep, which the squirrel hopes to relocate by their smell. For a home the western gray enlarges an old woodpecker or flicker hole, or else builds a leaf-and-twig nest far out on the branch ends of a large tree. Its warning call, a husky bark, is occasionally heard in the vicinity of the oak woodlands. The western gray is said to be less agile in the trees than the smaller native squirrels, and to become easy prey for the marten if it leaves the open Transition Zone woods for the denser Canadian Zone forests.

Dusky-footed wood rat *(Neotoma fuscipes)*
The dusky-foot is a large, dark wood rat, about sixteen inches (406 mm) long. Its round, short-haired tail is almost as long as its head and body. Its coat is blackish brown above and white below on both body and tail.

The dusky-footed wood rat lives mainly in the drier parts of the chaparral, the streamside thickets, and the open woods of the valleys east of the Oregon Coast Range, but reaches the coast itself in southern Oregon. This member of the pack rat tribe is the master builder amongst the wood rats, constructing large conical apartment buildings up to six feet (183 cm) in height. Some of these are tree houses; some are built on the ground around shrubs or logs. The materials used are sticks, bones, bark, cans, leaves, moss, and so on. Inside chambers contain cup-shaped nests or food stores. The wood rat eats mostly greens, but also some fruits, nuts, and seeds. There are trails leading from lodges to feeding grounds and also between lodges, although there are rarely many residences located in any one area.

ALSO LOOK FOR: Vagrant shrew
Coast mole
California ground squirrel
Golden-mantled ground squirrel
Piñon mouse
Gapper red-backed mouse
Creeping vole

40

Lowland
Meadow
and Field

The essence of this association—lowland meadow and field—is the presence of grasses and herbaceous (nonwoody) plants, together with a fairly high level of moisture. Such an association would include the valley farmlands, the old fields, and the few remaining patches of native moist prairie in the Puget Sound lowlands. Here climatic conditions would be those of the Humid Transition Life Zone (see under "Coastal Forest"). Some areas of the Northwest's interior— irrigated fields, ditch borders, and roadside verges—are also representative of this habitat type, even though they experience much wider temperature variations and lie in different life zones. Thus, some noncoastal species are also considered animals of lowland meadow and field.

Sorex vagrans

Vagrant shrew *(Sorex vagrans)*
A tiny four-inch (102 mm) shrew, the vagrant adult weighs only about one-quarter ounce (7 to 8 g). Its coat color is usually grayish below and brownish above, generally lighter and ruddier in summer.

The vagrant is probably the most common of our shrews, both in population and in number of habitats utilized. It lives out its eighteen months or so of life full tilt, consuming approximately its own weight in food each twenty-four hours. Like the other small land shrews, the vagrant digs to some extent in the topsoil, but its maze of tunnels and runways is to be found just under logs, leaf litter, or fallen grass. Its short sighted approach to finding food is to rush along, exploring every part of its environs, its long snout sweeping until its sensitive vibrissae (whiskers) touch something. The smell will then indicate whether that something is good to eat or not.

Coast mole *(Scapanus orarius)*
The coast mole looks just as you would expect a mole to look with its black velvety fur, very scantily haired snout and tail, and powerful broad forepaws, well adapted for digging. Its total length is 6½ to 7 inches (165 to 178 mm).

The coast mole is usually to be found in meadow, pasture, and deciduous jungle. It leads an almost completely subterranean life in a maze of tunnels and burrows. It rarely throws up the dirt ridges that would be the result of tunneling just below the surface of the ground, but molehills are common, serving as outlets for soil excavated from tunnels. The molehill is conical rather than fan-shaped like that of the pocket gopher *(Thomomys),* and there is no hole or exit plug in it. Worms, insects, and spiders form the bulk of the mole diet, with succulent roots and other soft vegetation as tasty supplements. The

42

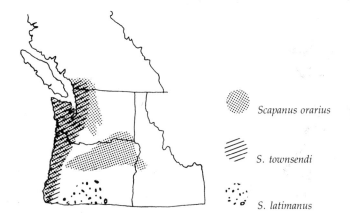

Scapanus orarius

S. townsendi

S. latimanus

mole is not a sociable animal most of the year, but with the coming of spring there are family cares, usually revolving around a brood of three young. These are raised in an underground nest of grass, leaves, and rootlets, and at the end of two months are almost adult.

At 8½ to 9 inches (216 to 229 mm) in length, the Townsend mole (*S. townsendi*) is simply a larger version of the coast mole, and is actually more restricted to coastal areas than the latter. The Townsend is similar in habits as well as in appearance but does tend to stay in the wet lowland areas and out of the scrub, deciduous woods, or drier upland meadows.

The broad-footed mole (*S. latimanus*) is intermediate in size between the moles described above but has forepaws as wide as the

COAST MOLE (*Scapanus orarius*)

CALIFORNIA GROUND SQUIRREL *(Spermophilus beecheyi)*

larger Townsend. Its tail is also richer in number of hairs. The broad-footed mole occupies the drier country found primarily in the soft, light, even sandy soils of open valleys and semiarid mountains. Its life zone range stretches all the way from Upper Sonoran to Hudsonian.

California ground squirrel,
Beechey ground squirrel *(Spermophilus beecheyi)*

The California is king among the ground squirrels. It measures about eighteen inches (457 mm), of which some seven inches (178 mm) are long bushy tail. The pelage is a lightly dappled gray brown. A gray "cape" is interrupted by a dark triangular band spreading from the neck to the mid-back.

The California ground squirrel will live in several life zones as

44

Spermophilus beecheyi

long as the weather is reasonably mild, generally in areas of grasses or grains or in very open woods. Its habits almost place it in a category between ground squirrels and tree squirrels. It is a good climber and does take to the trees to harvest fruits and nuts. It can "churr" like a squirrel or whistle like a marmot. On sloping or well-drained ground it digs its burrow. This underground home has several branches but only one entrance, beside a rock or a tree root. Stumps and boulders are used as lookout posts. It has not yet been established whether the California ground squirrel is a hibernator. It is, however, an animal whose range extension can almost be documented from one year to the next. It is said to have crossed the Columbia River in 1912 and is apparently spreading successfully up through south central Washington.

WESTERN HARVEST MOUSE *(Reithrodontomys megalotis)*

Reithrodontomys megalotis

Western harvest mouse *(Reithrodontomys megalotis)*
This little mouse (5½ to 6 inches, 140 to 152 mm) is brownish above and whitish below, including its tail. It is sometimes confused with the deer mouse (some forms of which have a similar coloration but a larger size) or with the house mouse (whose tail is more naked and not white on the bottom). The most definitive characteristic is the outer surface of the upper incisors; of the three groups, only those of the harvest mouse will have grooves.

The western harvest mouse lives in the drier locations, mainly in the interior and in the Upper Sonoran Life Zone, but within this area it seeks out the dense, moist vegetation of ditch banks, field borders, marshes, and meadows. It moves about at night, using the runways of the diurnal meadow mice, or making its own network under thick grass and weeds. It may also use the burrows of other species but is better known for the construction of its own globular or cup-shaped nests of dry grass, sometimes lined with plant down. These nests may be hung in the vegetation like a bird's nest, or placed on the ground in a sheltered spot. Primarily a seed eater, the harvest mouse also feeds on fruits and stem cuttings. Some food is stored away against the arrival of inclement weather, although this mouse does remain active throughout the year. It is quite a prolific little mammal, bearing litters of four to six young several times a year.

Western jumping mouse *(Zapus princeps)*
Jumping mice are a special breed with a family all their own. The western jumping mouse measures 9 to 9½ inches (229 to 241 mm), much of that belonging to its long, tapering bicolored tail. Following the pattern of the saltatorial (jumping) animal, it has small forefeet but large and strongly developed hind limbs. Its coat is quite distinctive

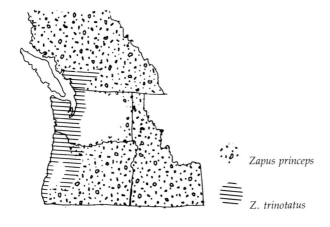

Zapus princeps

Z. trinotatus

with a dark dorsal band grading into an olive-tinged yellow on the sides and white underparts. The upper incisors are grooved.

The western jumping mouse likes the vicinity around water, either wet grassland or ravine thicket of the Transition Life Zone or higher elevations. Its usual method of locomotion is by short hops through the grass, using its long tail for balance. Should it be startled, however, it can take up to six feet (183 cm) in a bound, and then continue bounding in zigzags. Reputedly, you can hear a jumping mouse rustling and thudding through the grass. Occasionally it will use the runways of voles, but it is also a trailblazer in its own right. Piles of grass stems cut in long sections are deposited here and there along the paths. The grass is cut primarily for its seeds, the main food of the jumping mouse. In summer the western jumping mouse lives in shallow burrows or holes under rocks or logs, emerging to feed mainly after dark. In August it begins accumulating layers of fat, and by

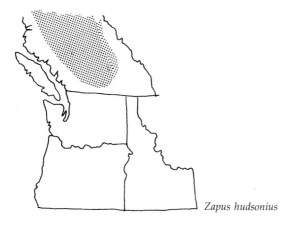

Zapus hudsonius

mid-September has retired to a deeper burrow several feet underground. Here it spends the winter in hibernation, curled up in a tight ball in a snug grass nest. The spring awakening is followed by breeding, and there will be one or two litters per year.

The Pacific jumping mouse (*Z. trinotatus*, pl. 2) is much the same size, but its yellow sides and dark back are more sharply demarcated. Both species exhibit similar behavior and habitat choice, but the Cascade Mountain crest forms the principal divider between their geographic locations.

The meadow jumping mouse (*Z. hudsonius*) is smaller than the other two by an inch (25 mm) or so, but similar in habits and habitat. Always partial to water, the meadow jumping mouse likes marshy spots, streamside habitat, or moist brushy and grassy areas. It is said to bear but one litter annually, and that in June.

ALSO LOOK FOR: Columbian ground squirrel
Northern pocket gopher
Meadow voles

Lowland Stream Bank, Lakeshore, and Marsh

The association of lowland stream bank, lakeshore, and marsh is one step beyond moist meadow or moist scrub. It consists of fresh or brackish water and the bordering wetlands, which often support a lush growth of herbaceous vegetation. Characteristic marsh plants are sedges, cattails, and reeds. Such woody plants as willows and cottonwoods thrive in the vicinity of water. Here one might also find cedar, dogwood, birch, aspen, or alder. Muskrat, beaver, and certain other animals often seek this habitat—whether it is located on the coast or in the interior, whether it is in the Transition or Upper Sonoran Life Zone, whether its temperature range is extreme or moderate.

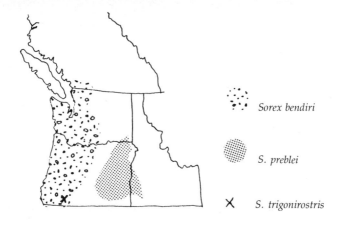

Sorex bendiri

S. preblei

X   S. trigonirostris

Marsh shrew, Pacific water shrew *(Sorex bendiri)*
At first glance, the marsh shrew (pl. 2) looks like a lowland counterpart of the water shrew *(S. palustris)*. The marsh shrew is also about six inches (152 mm) in length and blackish in color. Unlike the water shrew, however, it is not much lighter ventrally, except for the Olympic Peninsula subspecies, and possesses an all-dark tail.

The marsh shrew inhabits the lower elevation swamps, bogs, sluggish streams, and very wet woods. Its life zone range is Humid Transition and lower Canadian. Here it pursues a rather typical "shrewish" existence (very energetic but short-lived) under logs, in tall grass, and in the alder thickets of the most moist and muddy places.

The small Malheur or Preble shrew *(S. preblei)* also likes the soggy places but seeks them out in the Upper Sonoran and Arid Transition life zones, reaching an altitude of about 5,000 feet (1,524 m)

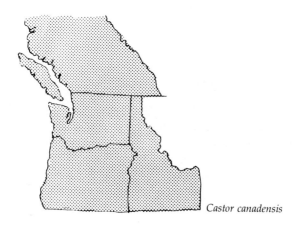

Castor canadensis

BEAVER *(Castor canadensis)*

in the mountains of northeastern Oregon and southeastern Washington.

The Ashland shrew *(S. trigonirostris)* is likewise a small shrew, as well as a short-tailed one, found only in the Ashland area of Oregon below 3,500 feet (1,067 m). In that region it is found alongside streams and where vegetation is damp, but sometimes on the drier slopes as well.

Beaver *(Castor canadensis)*

I fancy this heavyweight of the North American rodents needs little description. Not so easily observable in the wild, the beaver has been illustrated so often, most people would readily recognize the broad, flat, scaly tail and the large, webbed hind feet, which leave such distinctive tracks in wet mud. The beaver measures about forty inches (1,016 mm) and usually weighs forty to fifty pounds (18 to 23 kg)— sometimes sixty pounds (27 kg) or more.

BEAVER *(Castor canadensis)*

Streams, lakes, and ponds from the lowlands up into the Canadian Zone are the places to find beavers, or at least signs of their presence. The animals themselves emerge for work mainly after sundown. If they live in streams where the water is swift and deep, they usually dig burrows in the banks. In other aquatic habitats they opt for lodges built of sticks, logs, debris, and mud, perhaps twelve feet (366 cm) across at the base and rising several feet above the water. In both cases, the entrances are under the surface, but the central nest chambers are snug and dry above the waterline. Beavers are fairly unusual rodents for the strength of their family ties. In the late winter male and female mate, and about May some four beaver kits are born, already furred. A typical lodge family consists of mother, father, and the litters of two successive years.

Dams are built where it is necessary to deepen the water for the protection of lodges or food stores. In the fall, a winter's supply of twigs and branches are brought down and stored in the soft mud of the pond floor to provide bark and cambium as food after the freeze-over. In the summer more green vegetation is eaten. Preferred food species are aspen, birch, alder, cottonwood, and willow, plus pond lilies, cattails, sedges, and the like. The energetic beaver is quite capable of felling trees a foot (30 cm) or more in diameter, and quite speedily too. To do so, it sits on its hind legs, using its tail as a prop, and gnaws out bite-sized chunks with its strong incisors. Piles of these "beaver chips"

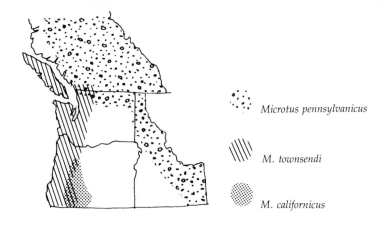

Microtus pennsylvanicus

M. townsendi

M. californicus

and the tooth-marked cuts in the tree trunks distinguish the work of a beaver from that of an axe. To get from home pond to feeding area, the beaver may dig out channels rather than go overland. It is capable of swimming long distances under water, using its hind feet for propulsion and its tail as a rudder. The paddlelike tail can also be slapped against the water or ground to send a signal to fellow beavers.

Beavers have played a great role in the history of this continent. They have actually created mountain valleys, distributed water runoff, raised water tables, made new habitat for fish and waterfowl, and stimulated the regrowth of vegetation. They were heavily trapped when the West was first explored and exploited and their fur was highly prized, particularly for beaver hats. Their numbers reached the point of near extinction by the late 1800s, from which they are now slowly recovering. Surely the benefits of their presence offset some local destruction, such as flooding of pastures and damage to fruit trees.

Meadow vole, Pennsylvania meadow mouse *(Microtus pennsylvanicus)*
The meadow vole (pl. 2) is about seven inches (178 mm) of mouse, 25 percent of which is tail. It is dark brown above, grayish white below, and represents the epitome of vole conformation—blunt nose, small ears, and short tail.

The meadow vole is an inhabitant of marshy areas and damp meadows with lush vegetation. Throughout the greenery meander its well-used runways, marked here and there by piles of feces and cut stems and blades of grass. Sometimes the trails end at the water's edge, for the meadow vole is an accomplished swimmer. It lives in burrows in the damp earth, and like most voles, subsists almost entirely on succulent greens. It is a prolific breeder, producing four or more litters

MONTANE VOLE (*Microtus montanus*)

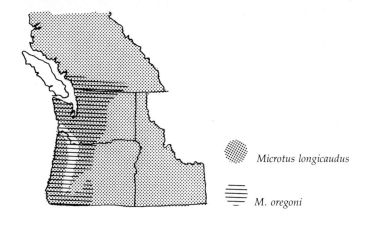

Microtus longicaudus

M. oregoni

a year. The young female is capable of reproducing at the age of only one month. Meadow voles are frequently found in dense colonial groupings. As with other species of *Microtus, pennsylvanicus* populations may show large buildups every four to six years, followed by a crash and then a rebuilding, in a continuing cyclic pattern.

The meadow vole has the greatest range of any *Microtus,* extending from one side of the North American continent to the other and from Alaska down into some of the southern states. I rescued one once from a swimming pool filter on Long Island, New York. There are a number of *Microtus* species so similar in appearance and habits that it is not a task for the amateur to attempt to differentiate them. The long-tailed vole *(M. longicaudus),* with a relatively long bicolored tail, lives mainly in the wet meadows and streamsides of the Canadian Life Zone and down into the Transition. It seldom makes runways. The Townsend vole *(M. townsendi)* prefers the swamps and wet grasslands of the coastal lowlands where there is dense cover. It is a large mouse (nine to ten inches, 229 to 254 mm) with a relatively long tail and is active day and night in its maze of trails concealed by the vegetation. It is not averse to living in fairly well-populated areas or in close proximity to man, yet is apparently uninterested in his buildings or food supplies. I flush panic-stricken Townsend voles whenever I run the mower through the rough grass beyond the limits of that small patch I labor to maintain as true lawn at my home on Vashon Island, Washington. The other day I picked up an old tarp lying for some months beside the vegetable garden. Underneath, amidst the expected complement of slugs, sowbugs, and earwigs, was a veritable labyrinth of runs, each one a shallow tunnel without a top.

The montane vole *(M. montanus)* belies its name. It is a short-tailed meadow mouse, dark brownish above, dark grayish beneath,

CREEPING VOLE *(Microtus oregoni)*

measuring 6 to 6½ inches (152 to 165 mm). It lives mainly in the tule marshes, ditch banks, and wet grasslands of the Upper Sonoran and Arid Transition life zones but spreads widely into sagebrush areas, especially during times of peak population (as is true to a lesser extent for the long-tailed vole). The montane vole shares its habitat and narrow trails with harvest mice, vagrant shrews, and muskrats. The gray-tailed vole *(M. canicaudus)* occupies the grasslands and pastures of northwestern and north central Oregon, just crossing into Washington in Clark County. Formerly considered a subspecies of *montanus,* it may be distinguished by the yellowish shading of its coat and lighter grayish belly.

The creeping vole *(M. oregoni),* also known as the Oregon meadow mouse, is a small, short-tailed mouse, 5 to 5½ inches (127 to 140 mm) long, which may occupy marshes and riverbanks but generally seeks a drier habitat than its relatives—open grassy areas, deciduous woods, and brushy areas. Here it constructs small tunnels among the grass roots, eats bulbs, roots, stems, and leaves, and makes globular nests of dry grass. Another vole of somewhat drier ground, but more restricted geographically, is the California vole *(M. californicus).* Moist, fresh dirt thrown out of its burrows onto dry ground, and pathways snaking through the short, dry grass often advertise its presence. An inhabitant primarily of the Upper Sonoran Life Zone, it lives on grassy valley slopes and dry upland meadows.

56

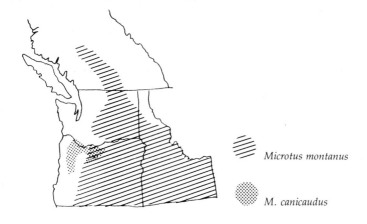

Microtus montanus

M. canicaudus

Muskrat *(Ondatra zibethicus)*

The muskrat (pl. 3) is so named for a pair of musk glands located on its lower abdomen. It is a rodent of some twenty to twenty-four inches (508 to 610 mm) in length, a little less than half of that devoted to a scaly tail, hairless and flattened on either side. The eyes and ears are small. The forefeet are also small, but the hind are large with partly webbed toes fringed with hair. A beautiful coat of thick, soft brown fur is almost concealed by long, stiff guard hairs.

Any water is home to the muskrat, but usually freshwater, and particularly the slow-moving streams or the still water of marshes, swamps, and ponds, from the Upper Sonoran into the Canadian Life Zone. In streams muskrats frequently live in bank burrows; in more open waters they often build dome-shaped houses reminiscent of beaver lodges, except that the materials used are mud, cattails, rushes,

Ondatra zibethicus

and other soft aquatic plants, rather than wood. These homes contain several underground entrances and a single chamber above water level with a nest of shredded leaves, an accommodation for a family of six to eight. Occasionally muskrats actually share beaver lodges with their owners. Usually, two to three litters, each with about half a dozen young, bless a muskrat family every year.

The muskrat feeds mainly on the tender basal parts of aquatic plants, supplementing this diet with mussels, snails, tadpoles, and the like. The muskrat knows how to live well and may do its feasting while floating on a raft of water plants. It is active all winter and can swim long distances under the ice, as well as under open water. This rodent can be observed abroad during the day, but the time of its greatest activity is night or twilight. The principal enemy of the muskrat is man, who covets a lovely fur so dense it can keep its owner dry under water; after man ranks the mink.

ALSO LOOK FOR: Vagrant shrew
Pygmy shrew
Snowshoe hare
Western harvest mouse
Jumping mice

Montane Forest and Clearing

The montane forest covers two life zones: the Canadian and the Hudsonian. This forest ascends the mountainsides from the upper edge of the Transition woodlands to almost timberline–from about 3,000 feet (914 m) to approximately 7,000 feet (2,134 m). (The montane forest begins at a lower altitude on the western slopes of the Cascades than on the eastern side.) Winters are moderately cold to cold, with a good snowfall. Summers are generally warm in the daytime, but are always cool at night and in shaded areas. Although rarely extremely dry, this forest does experience considerable variation in precipitation, averaging fifty inches (127 cm) annually. The wetter western slopes support a somewhat different species composition than the drier eastern slopes. Some of the kinds of trees you could expect to find are Engelmann spruce and western larch, several of the true firs and Douglas fir, western and mountain hemlock, Alaska cedar, western white and whitebark pines, lodgepole pine, alder and maple, juniper and mountain ash. Also look for rhododendron, wild currant, and huckleberry. Forest clearings usually offer the cover of stumps and fallen logs.

Sorex obscurus

Dusky shrew *(Sorex obscurus)*
The dusky is a medium-small shrew (pl. 3) about 4½ inches (114 mm) in length. Its coat is reddish brown above (darker in winter) and grayish brown below.

Without a doubt, most of the shrews are a clannish lot and make it difficult for anyone short of an expert to tell their species apart. The dusky shrew is similar to the vagrant, with which it was once lumped, but is partial to the moist places, or at least to the vicinity of water in forests and clearings, leaving the meadows to its wandering cousin. Either species may be found at a low or a high elevation, but the vagrant shrew is rarer in the high mountains, the dusky more common in montane and alpine habitats. It may roam onto the drier hillsides and heather-covered ridges. Its tiny tracks can be seen on the snow in winter, for like all shrews, the dusky has a high rate of metabolism, which drives it into activity and the search for invertebrate meat every two to three hours, day and night, winter and summer. About six young shrews are born in summer, frequently in a dry grass nest carefully placed in a rotten log.

Water shrew *(Sorex palustris)*
At six inches (152 mm) total length, the water shrew (pl. 4) is a large member of the shrew family. It also has quite a handsomely distinctive coat: the hairs on the back are blackish with frosting at the tips, those on the underparts are whitish, the color contrast carried out the full length of the tail. On the outer side of each hind foot is a fringe of stiff hairs that converts the foot to a paddle.

Though rarely seen, the water shrew is not uncommon in the cold streams and lakes of the Canadian and Hudsonian zones. It is a treat indeed to catch sight of one and watch its antics. It can trap air

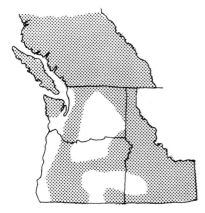
Sorex palustris

under its feet and literally skate or run across the surface of the water. Its thick fur also traps air, so that it dives in the midst of an air bubble, kicking its feet rapidly to overcome the buoyancy. It then searches along the stream bottom with its flexible snout and sensitive vibrissae for snails, leeches, tadpoles, larval invertebrates, and tiny fish to satisfy its ravenous appetite. As soon as its feet stop moving, the water shrew pops up to the surface, quite dry. Like other shrews, it lives about eighteen months, active periodically night and day and even under the ice in winter.

Red-tailed chipmunk *(Eutamias ruficaudus)*
At nine inches (229 mm) or a little more, the red-tailed chipmunk is a moderately large chipmunk, intermediate in size between the yellow-pine and the Townsend. In coloration—including the bright rufous

Eutamias ruficaudus

Glaucomys sabrinus

underside of the tail—it is very like the yellow-pine. Within its geographic range the red-tailed chipmunk seeks the dense coniferous forests just as the Townsend does further west. Both overlap portions of the yellow-pine chipmunk's range, but each fills a separate ecological niche. In the Rocky Mountains the red-tailed chipmunk may also be found in the stunted pine and spruce zone just below timberline.

Northern flying squirrel *(Glaucomys sabrinus)*

The northern flying squirrel *(frontispiece)* is 11½ to 12 inches (292 to 305 mm) long. It has beautiful soft, silky fur, gray above and creamy below, and large dark eyes. The gray tail is flat and used mainly as a rudder. There is a fur-covered fold of skin between each front and hind leg which can be stretched to give this squirrel its gliding abilities.

　　The northern flying squirrel is the only nocturnal squirrel in the Pacific Northwest and for that reason is rarely seen, although it is not uncommon. If you could watch, you would see it run up one tree, launch itself downward in a glide of up to fifty yards (46 m) or more, and end with an upward swoop on the lower level of another tree. It prefers old woodpecker holes in hollow trees, but any tree cavity, or even a moss or leaf nest, may be used. Tree hole dens are usually lined with shredded bark. Here a single litter, usually of three little squirrels, is born in May or June. The young will have learned to glide short distances by the time they are two months old. The flying squirrel eats a variety of forest foods, including bark, insects, and bird eggs, but is fondest of fungi in summer and lichen in winter. Not one to hibernate, it is out gliding quietly through the forest on cold winter nights, liable to become prey for one of the larger owls or other nocturnal predators.

Red squirrel *(Tamiasciurus hudsonicus)*

The red squirrel has a length of thirteen to fourteen inches (330 to 356

RED SQUIRREL *(Tamiasciurus hudsonicus)*

mm). All year it is dressed in a coat that is reddish gray above and whitish below.

The red squirrel lives in the coniferous forests of the Transition, Canadian, and Hudsonian life zones. It is out and about daytimes, winter or summer. As fall approaches, it becomes most active and vociferous, with quite a repertoire of barking, chattering, and scolding notes. This is the season when territories become rigidly defended. The squirrel's territory, averaging somewhere around 2½ acres (1 ha), covers the area in which it works feverishly to harvest and cache cones, either underground or in log or tree holes. Preferred cones are those of the Douglas fir, as well as pines. Gradually through

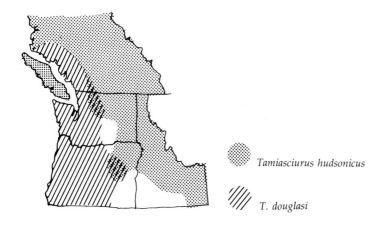

Tamiasciurus hudsonicus

T. douglasi

the course of the winter these cones will be reclaimed and eaten in a manner reminiscent of a human dealing with an ear of corn—the cone is held in the forepaws and rotated while the teeth are used to shuck the scales and eat the seeds until only a bare core remains. Favorite feeding stations can be identified by the mounds of scales and cores heaped around them. The conifer seed diet is supplemented with fruits, nuts, fungi, insects, buds, and flowers. The red squirrel may nest in tree cavities or balls of grass arranged in the branches. Usually a litter of some five young are born in the spring, and perhaps a second one in the early fall. Its principal enemies are martens, goshawks, and horned owls.

The Douglas squirrel or chickaree (*T. douglasi, cover photo*) looks not unlike the red, but is more dusky olive on the back and yellowish underneath. Both squirrels have much the same life-style, but the Douglas is found in the southwestern and coastal parts of the Pacific Northwest; the red, in the northern and eastern portions. The vigorous scolding or chattering of the Douglas squirrel is a common sound in the woods, its notes just a little less harsh than those of the red squirrel. The Douglas may also have a tree-hole nest, or may construct a round twig-needle-and-bark nest at least a foot (30 cm) in diameter, lined inside with bark.

ALSO LOOK FOR: Trowbridge shrew
Masked shrew
Water shrew
Shrew-mole
Snowshoe hare
Yellow-pine chipmunk
Townsend chipmunk
Golden-mantled ground squirrels
Mountain beaver
Gapper and western red-backed mice
Heather vole
Creeping vole
Western jumping mouse
Porcupine

PLATE 1

DEER MOUSE *(Peromyscus maniculatus)*

GAPPER RED-BACKED MOUSE *(Clethrionomys gapperi)*

SHREW-MOLE *(Neurotrichus gibbsi)*

PLATE   2

PACIFIC JUMPING MOUSE *(Zapus trinotatus)*

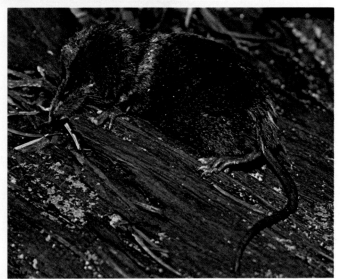

MARSH SHREW *(Sorex bendiri)*

MEADOW VOLE *(Microtus pennsylvanicus)*

PLATE 3

MUSKRAT *(Ondatra zibethicus)*

DUSKY SHREW *(Sorex obscurus)*

PLATE 4

WATER SHREW (*Sorex palustris*)

OLYMPIC MARMOT (*Marmota olympus*)

PLATE 5

COLUMBIAN GROUND SQUIRREL
(Spermophilus columbianus)

HEATHER VOLE *(Phenacomys intermedius)*

CASCADE GOLDEN-MANTLED GROUND SQUIRREL *(Spermophilus saturatus)*

PLATE 6

WHITE-TAILED JACKRABBIT *(Lepus townsendi)*

TOWNSEND GROUND SQUIRREL *(Spermophilus townsendi)*

PLATE 7

BLACK-TAILED JACKRABBIT *(Lepus californicus)*

PLATE 8

LEAST CHIPMUNK *(Eutamias minimus)*

WHITE-TAILED ANTELOPE SQUIRREL *(Ammospermophilus leucurus)*

Boulder Field and Talus Slope

Boulder fields and talus slopes are not confined to the upper elevations but are most common there–in the Hudsonian Life Zone and up above timberline in the Arctic-Alpine. This last is a barren world of exposed rock and windswept ridges where only a few low plants like dwarf willow, juniper, and heather survive, and lichens coat the rocks. Winters are long (a good eight months) and very cold, summers are cool, and precipitation is high. Drop lower in elevation, away from the peaks, and the world is not quite so harsh. Scattered boulders and talus adjoin alpine meadows, and most of the small mammals forage in these meadows, though they seek cover among the rocks. Only the pika is an animal exclusively of the slide rock, but enough of the others are associated with this habitat to warrant its separate consideration here.

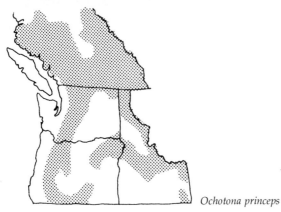

Ochotona princeps

Pika, coney *(Ochotona princeps)*
The pika looks rather like a guinea pig, with its round tailless body and round ears. It is some eight inches (203 mm) in total length. Its coat color varies considerably from a light grayish buff to a dark brown.

The pika is almost always found in rockslides and talus, usually in the mountains, but sometimes at elevations down to a few hundred feet (100 m or so). More often heard than seen, it produces a high-pitched "eep" or "eenk" familiar to most hikers and climbers. This is a warning note to fellow pikas, probably from a lookout atop a rock. As one naturalist (Bailey, 1936) has described the pikas, "on fur-cushioned feet they scamper over the roughest rocks, silent and surefooted, alert and keen of sight and hearing, and quick to dive below at the first sign of danger."

Shelter in the rocks and protective coloration are the pika's only defenses, for it is abroad and working during the daylight hours. One of my greatest pleasures on mountain hikes is to listen for the sharp note of the pika, and when I hear it anywhere close, to stand or sit motionless and watch. Seemingly curious pikas will pop out from under rocks to have a look, blending in so well they are not easily observable except when moving. If you do nothing to alarm them, they may come close enough for a photograph even without a telephoto lens, and close enough for you to see their whole bodies vibrate as they emit their peculiar alarm call.

Pikas seem particularly fond of thistles and lupines but eat any of the available broad-leafed greens and grasses. In the late summer and fall they have their busiest season—cutting plants, carrying them home crosswise in their mouths, and laying them out on the rocks to dry. If rain threatens the curing vegetation, it is quickly carried to shelter, for these piles of hay are the pikas' survival rations for the

PIKA *(Ochotona princeps)*

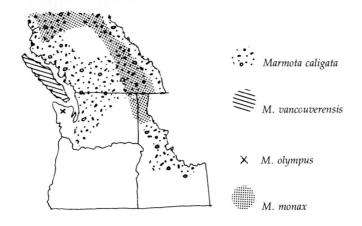

Marmota caligata

M. vancouverensis

X   *M. olympus*

M. monax

coming winter. Once cured, these haystacks—each a bushel (35 l) or more—are stored under rocks. The colonial pikas share pathways and central family nests in which one or two annual litters of altricial young are raised. The three or four youngsters of a litter must shoulder adult responsibilities at an early age. Though not yet fully grown, each must stake out its own territory and make its own haystacks in the face of the approaching winter. If you are in any doubt of the pika's lagomorph affinities, you have only to look at its small, round fecal pellets to know you are dealing with some sort of tiny rabbit.

Hoary marmot *(Marmota caligata)*
The hoary is a large marmot, some twenty-eight to thirty inches (711 to 762 mm) in length. It can weigh up to as many pounds (about 12 to 14 kg), but is more commonly less than half that amount. Its coat markings include a grayish white saddle over the back and shoulders and a light underbelly.

The hoary marmot is usually found at higher elevations, where alpine meadows are bordered by scattered rocks or talus. One might say that the rocks provide bed and the meadows board. Well-worn trails connect homes with meadows, to which the marmots move in the daytime to eat grasses and succulent alpine herbs. Flat-topped boulders provide lookouts, and every Cascades hiker knows how sharp and piercing is the warning whistle of the hoary marmot. It must be ever alert, for it has many predators, including cougar, bobcat, lynx, wolf, bear, coyote, and eagle. Still, a motionless pose often permits lengthy observation of marmots sunning atop rocks or ambling through greenery, foraging. The hoary retires into hibernation by mid-September and emerges again in April or May. It breeds soon afterwards and bears an average of three to five young in late spring, early summer. As slow to mature as it is in its other activities, the hoary is two years old before it reaches adulthood.

Two similar marmots living in isolated alpine and subalpine areas are the Vancouver marmot *(M. vancouverensis)* of Vancouver Island, and the Olympic marmot *(M. olympus, pl. 4)* of the Olympic Mountains of Washington. The Vancouver marmot is the smallest of the three, and said to be the quietest, seldom heard whistling to its fellows.

The woodchuck *(M. monax)* is a small, dark marmot, twenty-one to twenty-two inches (533 to 559 mm), with a reddish brown belly and upper legs. In the Pacific Northwest one looks for this marmot mainly in the Rocky Mountains and adjoining montane areas, in open parkland as well as alpine rockslides. It is also known as a quiet marmot, living in holes under rocks or in burrows frequently excavated at the base of a tree. Foxes, coyotes, and badgers are its principal enemies, though they find the woodchuck vulnerable only when outside its home.

ALSO LOOK FOR: Yellow-pine chipmunk
Yellow-bellied marmot
Golden-mantled ground squirrels
Bushy-tailed wood rat
Gapper red-backed mouse

Alpine Meadow, Stream, and Bog

Alpine meadows, streams, and bogs may be found in the Arctic-Alpine Life Zone but are probably most characteristic of the open areas of the Hudsonian, particularly towards its upper edge. Winters here are long and severe. Heavy snows cover the ground, accumulating to a height of thirty feet (9 m), and snowmelt rivulets and puddles often keep the ground wet until the early snows come again in late August and early September. The meadows are known for their colorful variety of flowering plants, which usually reach the height of bloom around early August. The names of just a few of these are anemone, spreading phlox, saxifrage, cinquefoil, dwarf willow, shooting star, bear grass, Indian paintbrush, avalanche lily, pentstemon, spring beauty, gilia, bitterroot, monkey flower, and alpine aster. During the short summer the sunny days may be warm, but the nights are chilly.

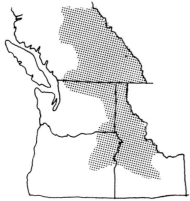

Spermophilus columbianus

Columbian ground squirrel (*Spermophilus columbianus*)
The Columbian is a large ground squirrel, about fourteen inches (356 mm) long. Four of these inches (102 mm) belong to its bushy tail. The upper parts are a grayish buff color, mottled with small white spots.

The Columbian ground squirrel (pl. 5) frequents grasslands at whatever elevation—thus meadows and parklands, pastures and grainfields, even the floor of the open pine forest. However, it prefers higher, moister country than such other ground squirrels as the Townsend and the Washington. The Columbian ground squirrel is usually colonial, and large populations may make pests of themselves in the grainfields and pastures. Next to stumps, logs, or stones they dig extensive burrow systems with several entrances. There are separate storage, sanitary, and nesting chambers, the nests lined with dry grass in which about four blind and toothless young are born after a twenty-four-day gestation period. The Columbian ground squirrel eats all types of plant material, some insects as well. It communicates with its fellows by means of sharp whistles or noisy chirping. Once again aestivation grades into hibernation, and consequently this ground squirrel spends a good seven to eight months curled up in a tight ball wrapped around by its tail, quite oblivious of the struggles for survival taking place over its head.

Northern pocket gopher (*Thomomys talpoides*)
The pocket gopher leads the same subterranean life as the mole and has smiliar fossorial adaptations, though a less extreme development of them: small eyes and ears, short fur, a relatively short and sparsely haired tail, long foreclaws, heavy shoulders, and small hips for turning in a tunnel. The northern pocket gopher is about eight inches (203 mm) in length and yellowish to grayish brown in color.

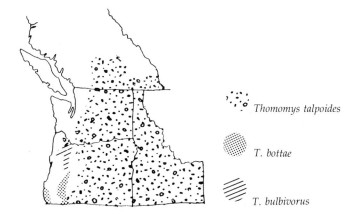

Thomomys talpoides

T. bottae

T. bulbivorus

The northern pocket gopher seeks semiopen areas with fairly deep, soft soil for burrowing, although a student of this accomplished digger reports it can go through almost anything but rock, moving an amazing amount of material in a short time. It digs with front claws, throwing the dirt behind it, then turns and shoves the loose dirt out of the burrow with its forelimbs and rather blunt head. One captive escaped its aquarium not once, but twice, by shoving a mound of dirt up against one edge and simply walking over. (Was it just luck, sheer perseverance, or actual cunning?) Thereafter it gnawed its way into baseboard and wall paneling, and only when hunger overcame all natural caution could it be lured into a baited trap and recaptured.

The northern pocket gopher is most common in mountain meadows, grassy prairies, dry slopes, and pine forest floors east of the Cascade crest. Sure signs of the gopher's presence are its earth mounds, differing from those of a mole in being more fan shaped, with a definite opening on one side. The last load of dirt pushed out forms a plug, and exits for surface feeding are also kept plugged. Other evidence of the gopher are the intertwining "ropes" of dirt found lying atop the ground in the spring, the remains of earth pushed up into the melting snow as the gopher moved from its snow tunnels into the ground. This animal remains active, burrowing through the snow if necessary, all winter long.

Gophers work mainly at night, but I have sat in a campground during the day and seen plants sink swiftly underground—one minute rooted and standing motionless, the next disappearing in a flash into a gopher tunnel whose owner is harvesting the leaves and bulbs or roots without ever having to surface. The gopher is a loner and quite aggressive towards other gophers except during the spring mating season. The burrow system of each animal usually includes a winding main

NORTHERN POCKET GOPHER *(Thomomys talpoides)*

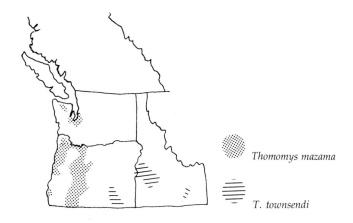

Thomomys mazama

T. townsendi

tunnel six to twelve inches (15 to 30 cm) below ground, deep nesting and storage chambers, and several side tunnels for feeding. Tunnels are frequently run alongside objects like logs. The pockets of the pocket gopher refer to the large fur-lined cheek pouches in which it can transport plant cuttings back to the storage areas. On uncultivated land this rodent can be beneficial. It aerates the soil, stimulates plant growth, prevents rapid water runoff, keeps down grass and weeds. On cultivated ground it can be a menace, eating mature plants, burying seedlings, clogging drainage ditches.

Pocket gophers cannot spread easily over unsuitable ground. Long-isolated populations exist, and have given rise to a number of new subspecies and even species, though these may vary little in appearance and even less in behavior in the eyes of any but the mammalogist. The Idaho and the Douglas *(Thomomys talpoides idahoensis* and *Thomomys t. douglasi,* respectively) are two now believed by some to represent full biological species because newer taxonomic methods are providing us a better understanding of characteristics such as karyotype, or chromosomal makeup. There are several well-recognized species of pocket gophers in the Pacific Northwest. The Botta pocket gopher *(T. bottae)* frequents southwestern Oregon. Separate populations of the larger, darker Townsend pocket gopher *(T. townsendi)* inhabit the fertile river bottoms of southeastern Oregon and southern Idaho. The small reddish brown Mazama or western pocket gopher *(T. mazama)* is found in western Oregon, including the Oregon Cascades, as well as in the Olympic Peninsula and the Puget Sound lowlands of Washington. The large, sooty brown camas pocket gopher *(T. bulbivorus),* with its white chin and protruding upper incisors, is restricted to Oregon's Willamette Valley.

Phenacomys intermedius

Heather vole, mountain heather vole *(Phenacomys intermedius)*
The heather vole (pl. 5), or mountain heather vole, is a medium-sized vole of about six inches (152 mm). It is ashy to brownish gray above and grayish white below, this contrast extending onto its short but slender and thinly haired tail.

As its name implies, this vole is a resident of the heather and huckleberry patches of the alpine habitat. It may be found at lower elevations, down to the Transition Life Zone, in grassy parkland and dry open forest of such species as lodgepole pine, but is an uncommon animal even among its preferred heather beds. It is known partly for its large, round nest, six to eight inches (15 to 20 cm) in diameter, composed of shredded snow grass, moss, and lichen. It builds the nest within or below the snow in winter, leaving it to be found atop the ground in spring. In summer the heather vole lives underground or in decaying timber. It is abroad day and night, but twilight is one of its most active times. No maker of trails, it sometimes chooses to travel in the runways of other voles. White heather, bear grass, bearberry, huckleberry, and lousewort are staple foods, along with various types of bark and lichen.

Water vole, Richardson vole, water rat *(Microtus richardsoni)*
The water vole is a meadow mouse of rat proportions (about eight inches, 203 mm), with rather long, coarse fur. It is dark brown above and dusky below, its medium-length tail also bicolored.

The water vole lives in the banks of cold mountain streams and in the marshes and meadows of the Canadian and Hudsonian life zones, particularly at higher elevations. It is semiaquatic, and its broad runways often connect burrows with small landings at the water's edge. Bank burrows may resemble miniature muskrat domiciles, hold-

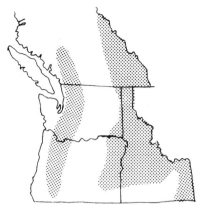

Microtus richardsoni

ing bulky nests of dry shredded grass. A hole in the ground, or beneath the snow in winter, may also serve as a home. The water vole is quite mobile in winter, tunneling through the snow over slopes it will find dry and impassable in summer. It eats blueberries, avalanche lilies, asters, clover, and other plants of its alpine habitat, turning more to roots, bulbs, and bark in winter. Like other meadow mice, the water vole frequently strews the stems of its food plants along its trails, marking spots where it spent some time in diurnal or nocturnal foraging.

Northern bog lemming, northern bog vole *(Synaptomys borealis)*
The northern bog lemming is a stout five-inch (127 mm) vole with a very short tail. Its longish woolly fur is grayish brown to brown above,

Synaptomys borealis

and dull gray below.

This lemming may be found in the cold, boggy alpine and subalpine meadows and muskegs. It is usually a scarce animal but is occasionally common in a particular area. It eats mainly grasses, sedges, and alpine plants, leaving piles of cuttings as well as feces along its well-marked runways. In summer it nests in an underground burrow and there bears its four or five young. In winter it may move to higher ground, to share the heathery habitat of the heather vole. Then the northern bog lemming builds spherical nests of dry grasses about eight inches (20 cm) in diameter. Though not a true lemming (a mouse of the genus *Lemmus)*, the bog lemming does undergo the same type of periodic fluctuation in population size as the former.

ALSO LOOK FOR: Dusky shrew
                     Hoary marmot
                     Gapper red-backed mouse
                     Meadow vole
                     Long-tailed vole
                     Pacific and western jumping mice

Open
Pine Forest

Open pine forest is a habitat that corresponds primarily to the arid, timbered portion of Merriam's Transition Life Zone. It is a forest of the interior, found from the lower east slopes of the Cascades eastward. Its usual elevation is about 1,000 to 3,000 feet (305 to 914 m). The winters in this forest are moderately cold, averaging below-freezing temperatures in January and February; the summers are quite warm. Winter snowfall may be heavy, but summers are dry, so the average annual precipitation is not more than twenty inches (51 cm). The predominant tree in this association is the ponderosa or yellow pine. Some of its associates are Douglas fir, western larch, and western birch. Since the yellow pine grows in open stands, the cover in its habitat is provided by rocks, fallen timber, or a variety of berry-bearing plants: chokecherry, serviceberry, snowberry, bearberry, salmonberry, raspberry, currant, etc. At their upper limit, yellow pines grade into lodgepole pines, which form dense stands when young but open up with maturity. Mountain parklands may have the character of very open pine forest.

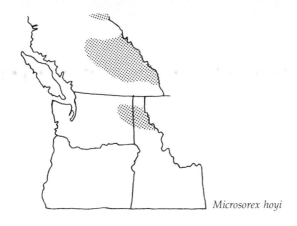

Microsorex hoyi

Pygmy shrew *(Microsorex hoyi)*
Being the smallest of the shrews, *Microsorex* thereby rates as the smallest of all North American mammals. It averages barely over three inches (76 mm) in total length, and its tail is a relatively small proportion of that. The fur is a grayish brown above, and gray below. I always delight in showing this wee beastie to museum visitors and having them marvel at its being a fully adult animal.

Little is known of the life history of the pygmy shrew other than its preference for drier areas than desired by the majority of shrews. It apparently selects open coniferous forest, grassy forest clearings, and parkland, although it can also be found in the wetter areas bordering meadows, marshes, lakes, and thickets.

Yellow-pine chipmunk *(Eutamias amoenus)*
A medium-sized chipmunk about eight inches (203 mm) long, the

Eutamias amoenus

YELLOW-PINE CHIPMUNK *(Eutamias amoenus)*

yellow-pine is bright in its colors. It has sharply contrasting black and white stripes set against a brown or gray brown background. The sides are brushed by varying degrees of rust, and the tail is rusty-colored underneath.

The name of this chipmunk indicates the areas of its prime abundance. However, it can also be found in mountain meadows and clearings, on logged or burned-over lands, and in other open places that are brushy or rocky. Since it prefers open woods, a characteristic growth pattern for yellow pine, this chipmunk is found among the yellow pines in the foothills of the eastern Cascades, and then again where the trees thin out towards the timberline. In the intervening zone (albeit with considerable overlap) one finds the Townsend chipmunk, which prefers the denser growth pattern of the fir and spruce forests. In the Olympic Mountains there is the same ecological separation, and the yellow-pine chipmunk may be found in open areas down to about 2,000 feet (610 m) but not in the dense forests which clothe the midslopes.

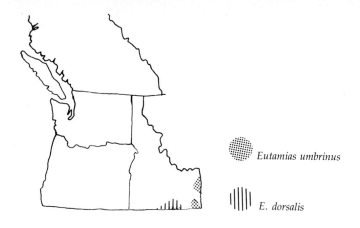

Eutamias umbrinus

E. dorsalis

The yellow-pine is diurnal, as all chipmunks are, but often rests quietly in the shade from midmorning till after midafternoon—when the sun is hot. It feasts on insects and any available plant food during the spring, turning more and more to seeds and grains as these ripen. One of its favorite nesting spots is a crevice in a granite rock surrounded by vegetation; otherwise it will use a short burrow under a tree root or a fallen log. It disappears underground with the coming of the first snows of winter and reappears in the spring to breed and bear a litter of about six young. Though naked and blind at birth, like most rodent babies, these youngsters are weaned at six weeks, reaching almost adult size by the end of the summer. The agile little yellow-pine chipmunk takes to climbing more readily than its cousins. Owing to both a greater abundance and a greater boldness, it is more frequently seen and heard than the other species—typically scampering along a log with its tail high in the air, or perched on a rock giving out shrill "chip, chip chip" notes and accenting each with a twitch of the tail.

Once, while resting against the bottom of a tree trunk at a trailside campsite, I watched amused as a chipmunk approached my backpack leaning against another tree some ten feet (3 m) away. The top flap was loosely fastened, no real obstacle to a daring animal drawn on by the delectable smell wafting from a trail snack of mixed nuts and raisins residing somewhere in the depths of the pack. Half a dozen times the chipmunk slipped in, emerged with cheeks crammed full of peanuts and raisins, ran a short distance, and buried its treasures in shallow depressions scratched out for that purpose. I have no doubt it would have continued till all were its property, but I felt it only right that we share. While the chipmunk was loading up once more, I walked up and put my hands down on the top of the pack. With a squeak of great alarm it scampered out one edge and dashed off across

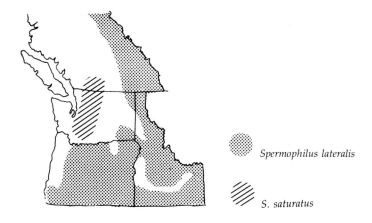

Spermophilus lateralis

S. saturatus

the clearing.

The yellow-pine chipmunk frequents much of the same country as the two species of golden-mantled ground squirrels but can easily be distinguished from the latter by the yellow-pine's smaller size and the presence of stripes on its face as well as along its sides.

Two species of chipmunks very restricted in their geographic distributions in the Northwest are the cliff chipmunk *(E. dorsalis)* and the Uinta chipmunk *(E. umbrinus)*. Look for the first—a medium-sized chipmunk of grayish hue, particularly on the rump—in the rocky juniper and piñon pine country of the extreme south-southeastern part of Idaho. The second—a quite large form with dull, almost indistinct stripes—lives along forest edges and in semiopen woods at points along the borders of southern and eastern Idaho.

Golden-mantled ground squirrel, Sierra Nevada
golden-mantled ground squirrel *(Spermophilus lateralis)*

The golden-mantled ground squirrel resembles a giant chipmunk, owing to its general coat color and the dark-light alternating stripes along each side. It is some ten inches (254 mm) long, however, and lacks the facial stripes which distinguish the little chipmunk.

In its behavior the golden-mantled ground squirrel is also quite like a chipmunk—especially the yellow-pine chipmunk, with which it often shares its habitat. However, the squirrel is less dependent on seeds and nuts, feeding on a fair amount of such other delicacies as mushrooms, roots, flowers, and berries. On several occasions I have seen one holding a bright yellow dandelion bloom in its forepaws, happily devouring the petals. The ground squirrel is also less arboreal than the chipmunk and is a true hibernator. Deposits of fat add to its weight in the fall, permitting it to retire underground and

GOLDEN-MANTLED GROUND SQUIRREL *(Spermophilus lateralis)*

to exist from about mid-September until the following May with all its bodily functions slowed to a minimum. Breeding occurs shortly after the reawakening, and there is one spring litter each year. The golden-mantled ground squirrel prefers to live in an underground burrow with protected and supported access. Thus, it is partial not

PORCUPINE *(Erethizon dorsatum)*

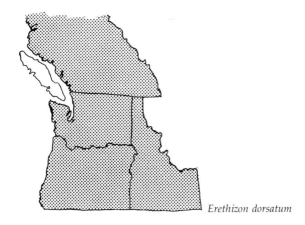
Erethizon dorsatum

only to pine forest but to mountain forest clearings with fallen trees and rocks, talus slides, logged or burned-over lands, and rocky meadows.

The Cascade golden-mantled ground squirrel *(S. saturatus, pl. 5)* is a slightly larger and duller replica of *S. lateralis* and may be found in the same type of habitat, pursuing the same activites. It is also seen in the company of the yellow-pine chipmunk. Both are residents and frequent visitors of campsites and picnic areas, happily accepting handouts or acting as a cleanup committee when the human feasting is over. The ground squirrel is characteristically observed running along the top of a log, sunning on a rock or a stump, or chasing others of its kind.

Porcupine *(Erethizon dorsatum)*

The porcupine is second only to the beaver in size among our rodents and weighs about half as much. Like the hoary marmot, it measures some twenty-eight to thirty inches (711 to 762 mm), but the average porky is the heavier, registering twenty to twenty-five pounds (9 to 11 kg) on the scales. It has small eyes and ears, heavy claws, and a short, muscular tail which serves as a prop in climbing. The familiar and dreaded stiff quills are interspersed among the long black-and-yellow-banded guard hairs of its coat, especially on the rump and tail.

The porcupine's quills are modified hairs which are loosely attached. When provoked, the porcupine erects them and with a slap of the tail drives them home (they are not hurled through the air). Back-slanting barbs at the tips then cause the quills to work in deeper. Assured of its spiny defense, the porcupine is slow in its movements and is neither timid nor cunning in its behavior. A tremendous number have fallen victim to automobiles because they failed to take alarm or to move off the roadway fast enough. A few predators—

mountain lion, bobcat, lynx, fisher, wolverine—can best the porcupine by attacking its spineless parts.

The porcupine inhabits all wooded areas but definitely prefers the dry, open coniferous forests of the interior Transition and Canadian life zones, not infrequently moving into brushy areas devoid of trees, or even onto the edges of the desert. It usually wanders at night, apparently at random, finding food as it goes—shrubs and herbs in summer, in winter the tender inner bark of the yellow pine and other conifers. It climbs up slowly to the "sugar zone," three to four feet (91 to 122 cm) below the top of the tree, and then girdles the trunk and upper branches to get the inner bark and cambium layer. The porcupine often remains a considerable time, even days, resting and feeding in one tree, a pile of its oval sawdustlike fecal pellets accumulating below, before making its slow descent backwards. Not only may it kill trees but may also damage cabins and camps because of its insatiable appetite for anything made salty by human (as well as animal) grease or sweat. I find it hard to imagine what it is the porky likes about certain essential materials it has been known to gnaw with gusto—rubber, plastic, wire insulation, and the like.

After a seven-month gestation period the female porcupine bears her one (sometimes two) young in May or June in a den in a rocky cliff or amid boulders. Interestingly, the young are well developed at birth, sporting teeth, open eyes, and even some short, soft spines which quickly harden. Their mother will care for them for another four to five months. Though generally silent, porcupines can converse in squeaky, querulous voices.

ALSO LOOK FOR: Broad-footed mole
Red and Douglas squirrels
Western gray squirrel
Columbian ground squirrel
Northern pocket gopher
Bushy-tailed wood rat
Gapper red-backed mouse
Heather vole

Dry Grassland

The dry grassland association is found in that belt of vegetation between the open pine forest and the desert sagebrush. The main floral component is native bluebunch wheatgrass. This association would include the grainlands of the Columbia Plateau and the prairies of the interior. The area where it is present corresponds closely to the arid timberless section of the Transition Life Zone. Very little of it has been left to native grasses, and the mammalian fauna is a composite of species extending down from the pine forest and up from the desert. In the dry grasslands summer temperatures are high and winter temperatures are quite cool. There is snow, but the total annual precipitation recorded is usually only ten to fifteen inches (25 to 38 cm).

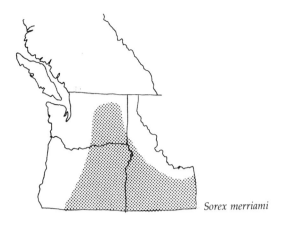

Sorex merriami

Merriam shrew *(Sorex merriami)*

One of the smallest of the shrews, the Merriam measures a scant 3½ to 4 inches (89 to 102 mm) in length. It is gray to grayish brown on the back but white on the throat, belly, feet, and underside of the tail.

This tiny shrew defies the moist habitat requirements of most of its relatives to live in the arid bunchgrass and sagebrush country. I do not believe it has yet fully divulged to any curious human just how it manages this. Secrets of its behavior as well as its physiology remain to be discovered and revealed to the world by some industrious student of shrew biology.

White-tailed jackrabbit *(Lepus townsendi)*

The white-tailed jackrabbit (pl. 6), true to its name, has an almost completely white tail. At about twenty-three inches (584 mm) total length, it is also larger than any other hare.

The white-tailed jackrabbit lives on the higher plateaus and hills of the Arid Transition Zone, moving down to share the sagebrush valleys with the blacktails in winter. In typical rabbit-hare fashion, the white-tail gets its food and water from succulent green vegetation in summer and turns to bark, buds, and twigs in winter, including in this case sagebrush and rabbit brush. If startled, it will bound off in tremendous erratic leaps and has been clocked moving at thirty-four miles (55 km) per hour. It leaps higher than the black-tail but does less zigzagging. The white-tailed jackrabbit makes only shallow forms, or hollows, in the ground in summer, but in winter burrows and tunnels deep in the snow. The young are born in the spring with a coat of brownish fur and are able to hop about within twenty minutes of their birth.

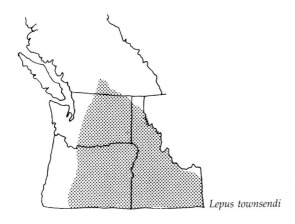

Lepus townsendi

Townsend ground squirrel *(Spermophilus townsendi)*
The coat of the Townsend ground squirrel (pl. 6) is a buffy gray with very pale dots over the back. Its head and body measure about 6½ inches (165 mm) in length, its tail 2 inches (51 mm).

The Townsend ground squirrel is partial to the mixed sagebrush and grassland areas of the hot, dry Upper Sonoran Life Zone. It is a highly gregarious squirrel, and where a sizable population occurs, the ground may be honeycombed with its burrows. These can extend many yards horizontally and have numerous openings. The excavated earth forms a rim or mound next to the burrow and from this vantage point the lookout watches and warns with its "lisping whistle" alarm call. All the alerted squirrels sit upright and motionless in picket pin position until the danger is over, or retreat quickly into their burrows if the threat seems great. They prefer green vegetation but also eat seeds, and are quite capable of becoming pests in fields of alfalfa and grain. In turn, they become food for many diurnal predators, such as badgers, weasels, skunks, bobcats, coyotes, hawks, and day-hunting owls. Since Townsend ground squirrels both aestivate and hibernate, they spend seven or eight months of each year underground, dormant.

There are several other ground squirrels of similar appearance and habits. The Washington ground squirrel *(S. washingtoni)* is darker, with more distinct spots. From the grasslands it ranges into the wheat fields and rocky hillsides of the Arid Transition Life Zone. Extending from there into the higher elevation grasslands, one finds the larger Richardson ground squirrel *(S. richardsoni)*, about twelve inches (305 mm), sporting a longer tail and cinnamon-colored underparts. Another large ground squirrel of meadows and field borders, particularly at higher elevations, is the Uinta ground squirrel *(S. armatus)*,

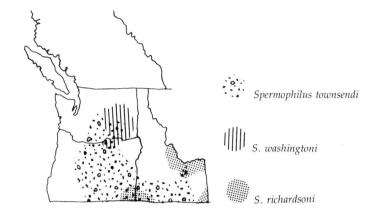

: :o: : *Spermophilus townsendi*

||||| *S. washingtoni*

S. richardsoni

found in southeastern Idaho. The Belding ground squirrel *(S. beldingi)* has a short tail that is reddish underneath. Also called the Oregon ground squirrel, it likes the eastern meadows, field borders, and edges of pine forest. The small, dappled Idaho ground squirrel *(S. brunneus)* inhabits the dry grasslands and rocky ridges in one area of western Idaho.

WASHINGTON GROUND SQUIRREL *(Spermophilus washingtoni)*

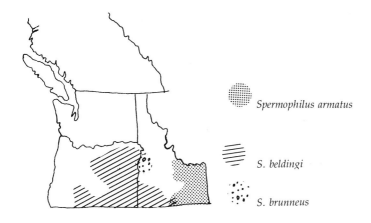

 Spermophilus armatus

S. beldingi

S. brunneus

ALSO LOOK FOR: Broad-footed mole
Black-tailed jackrabbit
Yellow-bellied marmot
Columbian ground squirrel
Northern pocket gopher
Great Basin pocket mouse
Sagebrush vole
Montane, California, and other voles

Sagebrush Desert

The sagebrush desert is the driest land of the Pacific Northwest, receiving ten inches (25 cm) or less of precipitation annually. This is a habitat you might first judge to be too harsh to support warm-blooded species in any numbers. You would be quite wrong. Small mammals abound here. This association has the characteristics of the Upper Sonoran Life Zone. Summers can be extremely hot, winters are generally moderately cold. The sagebrush, which gives its name to this association, enjoys the company of other xerophytic (dry-climate) plants: hopsage, black sage and winter fat, rabbit brush, greasewood, Russian thistle, cheatgrass, milk vetch, hawk's beard, mustard, and opuntia cactus, for example. The soil is frequently sandy and in some places almost pure sand.

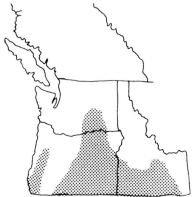

Lepus californicus

Black-tailed jackrabbit *(Lepus californicus)*

The black-tailed jackrabbit (pl. 7) measures about twenty-one inches (533 mm) from the tip of the nose to the tip of a tail that is black on top and a buffy gray underneath.

The black-tail is a hare mainly of the Upper Sonoran desert. However, it does tend to move into the surrounding Arid Transition grasslands and even outcompetes the white-tailed jackrabbit in that habitat. When its numbers reach a high point, the black-tailed jack may become a nuisance on fields of alfalfa, grain, and other crops. It is happy to add any of these cultivated plants to its diet of grass in summer; to buds, twigs, and bark in winter. It is a swift runner, using well-worn trails and runways. In the heat of the day the jackrabbit lies in a shaded depression or form. It moves and feeds at night, as well as in the evening and early morning hours. It may breed at almost any season and produces an average of five or six precocial young per litter.

Pygmy rabbit *(Sylvilagus idahoensis)*

The pygmy is a very small, silky-furred rabbit (about 10½ inches, 267 mm), paler in color than most other native rabbits. It possesses a tail that is totally gray instead of cottony white.

The home of the pygmy rabbit is dense sagebrush with associated rabbit brush and greasewood. It seeks areas where the soil is deep and not too hard packed, for it is a burrowing animal. The underground dwelling, often housing several individuals, has a number of entrances and exits. Each is about four inches (10 cm) in diameter and located next to a bush. A hungry badger may dig furiously at the hole on one side of a sagebrush plant whilst the rabbit pops out on the other side and escapes. Foraging is done not far from the burrow, or at least under cover of dense brush crisscrossed by the

94

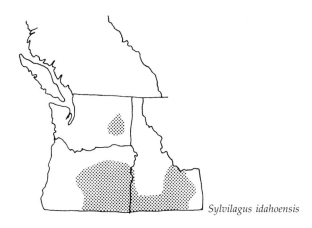

Sylvilagus idahoensis

rabbit's own trails and runways. The pygmy feeds on sagebrush both winter and summer, mainly during evening or nighttime hours. It is a fairly prolific breeder, producing its litters of altricial young spring and summer.

Least chipmunk *(Eutamias minimus)*
E. minimus (pl. 8) is indeed rather minimal in chipmunk terms, measuring only about seven inches (178 mm) in total length. It has a coat that is somewhat more grayish than that of other chipmunks, and a tail that is yellow on the underside.

PYGMY RABBIT *(Sylvilagus idahoensis)*

Eutamias minimus

A pert little inhabitant of sagebrush scrub, the least chipmunk is also found in alpine meadows and parkland in extreme eastern Idaho and northern British Columbia. It makes or borrows a burrow, or else uses a crevice among the rocks, and there bears its single litter of young in May. Sagebrush is used for shelter as well as for food. The least chipmunk dines largely on insects (especially larvae) in the spring, but turns more to fruits, foliage, and seeds by summer. In the fall a substantial number of seeds are brought home in bulging cheek pouches and cached. These food stores, rather than internal fat, are utilized by the chipmunk during brief wakeful periods in its long winter sleep and upon awakening in the early spring. The least is a shy and not very vocal chipmunk; it is usually seen, if at all, darting from the cover of one bush, heading for another.

White-tailed antelope squirrel,
antelope ground squirrel *(Ammospermophilus leucurus)*
This long, drawn-out appellation belongs to an extremely energetic and feisty ground squirrel of about nine-inch (229 mm) length. It is grayish brown with a white stripe on either side and a tail that is white underneath.

The white-tailed antelope squirrel (pl. 8) lives in the most barren, hot, dry spots amid the desert sagebrush and greasewood in southeastern Oregon and southwestern Idaho. Held up over its back, its tail flashes a white underside like the "flag" of an antelope—hence the name. This tail position also serves a purpose, for the white hairs do reflect heat off the body of the squirrel. When it is extremely hot, the white-tailed antelope squirrel retreats to its burrow underground or to the shade of the rocks to cool off by evaporation. Otherwise it is seen above ground, scampering rapidly from one bush to another, harvest-

Ammospermophilus leucurus

ing greens, cactus, berries, and green seeds in summer; ripe seeds and grains in winter. Those who have heard its voice describe the sound as a shrill, prolonged chip or a bubbling whistle. With regard to hibernation, the white-tailed antelope squirrel is strangely indecisive: it does lay on fat in the fall but does not regularly enter a dormant state.

Great Basin pocket mouse *(Perognathus parvus)*
This pocket mouse is a small seven-incher (178 mm) with a silky coat (olive gray above and buffy white below), a long silky tail, moderately long hind feet, and small ears.

The Great Basin pocket mouse prefers the sandy soils of the Upper Sonoran desert, extending also into the neighboring arid grasslands. Only after dark does it venture out of its extensive burrow

GREAT BASIN POCKET MOUSE *(Perognathus parvus)*

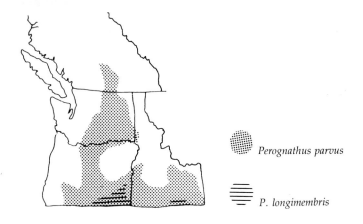

Perognathus parvus

P. longimembris

system—two to three feet (61 to 91 cm) deep—to feed mainly on the seeds of grasses and other desert plants. Especially in the spring, greens and insects add to its diet. Its forepaws quickly stuff food into capacious cheek pouches to carry home to mounded seed caches. Like other storing animals, the pocket mouse prefers to guard its own supplies and to lead a solitary life. Burrow entrances, which in any case are rather inconspicuous—small round holes sometimes under an inch (25 mm) in diameter—are usually plugged during the day against marauders and predators. The plugs also serve to maintain humidity levels.

Like the kangaroo rat, the pocket mouse may go its entire life without needing to drink water. It can extract sufficient moisture from the metabolizing of its food, as dry as ripe seeds may seem to us. Though it does not lose its sleek figure in the fall, the pocket mouse does retire to its burrow during the winter, passing the lean cold months in uncaring dormancy in its comfortable nest of dry grass, seed husks, weed twigs, and the like. A February or March emergence is followed by mating and the raising of one litter—two if seed germination has been good. Telltale signs of this clean, industrious little mouse are small burrow holes in open, sandy areas, a track of tail between tiny footprints, or shallow dustbathing wallows in the sandy soil. Another species, the little pocket mouse (P. longimembris), five inches (127 mm) in length, may be found in the southeastern corner of Oregon and extreme southern Idaho.

Given a little luck, watching a pocket mouse inside an aquarium can be as entertaining and educational as a mail-order ant farm or a section of bee-hive. There should be plenty of soil, of loose consistency so that excavations will not collapse. Usually at least one of the mouse's tunnels will be visible against the glass, perhaps even

Microdipodops megacephalus

during its construction. Maybe a food storage chamber will be revealed, however briefly, for the pocket mouse is continually busy revising and enlarging its burrow system. Here is a pet that does not require daily feeding, much less watering, and no cage cleaning either. I have more than once had the idea of going into business with a pocket mouse when I was hungry for unsalted sunflower seeds but too lazy to shell them. A perfect solution to this problem, I thought, would be to feed the seeds to the mouse and let it do the work. Think of those lovely caches of shucked seeds—of course, I would only take some of them.

Dark kangaroo mouse *(Microdipodops megacephalus)*
It is a small mouse (6 to 6½ inches, 152 to 165 mm) that bears this long Latin name. The dark kangaroo mouse is well colored for its desert habitat, being buffy gray above and creamy beneath. It is much like the larger kangaroo rat in appearance with its big head and eyes, ample cheek pouches, small forelegs, large strong hind legs, and balancing tail. A most distinctive feature is the tail: instead of being tufted at the tip, it is thickened in the middle, where a fat deposit is stored. The large back feet of the kangaroo mouse are clothed in dense fur. The tracks it leaves when hopping, showing hind feet only, look like miniatures of those of the kangaroo rat.

The dark kangaroo mouse loves the soft sandy soil amid the scrub sage in the very arid Upper Sonoran Life Zone. Like the pocket mouse, it usually stays in its plugged burrow during the day, emerging at night to feed. According to the best raconteur of its life that I have read, its favorite food is the seed of the abundant weed called blazing star. Its burrow lies about a foot (30 cm) below the surface and may extend five or six feet (152 to 183 cm) laterally. A more elaborate system including storage chambers is probably constructed before winter,

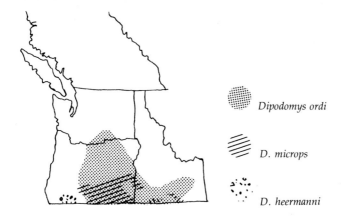

Dipodomys ordi

D. microps

D. heermanni

since in captivity this mouse has been seen burying pocketfuls of seeds when the supply was abundant. Four young constitute an average litter for the dark kangaroo mouse.

Ord kangaroo rat *(Dipodomys ordi)*
The Ord kangaroo rat is a large relative of the pocket mouse, a some-what more exaggerated model of the same basic design. Nine to ten inches (229 to 254 mm) in length, it has a large head with large black eyes but small ears, long hind feet, a long tufted tail with wider white than dark stripes, and a coat that is yellow buff above and white underneath.

      The Ord kangaroo rat is at home in the open sandy areas of the Upper Sonoran desert where the vegetation is sparse. Never a-broad during the daytime or in winter, it is a most efficient forager when active. Cheek pouches are rapidly filled with quantities of seeds to be emptied later into subterranean caches (a bushel, 35 l, or more not uncommon) by a quick pressing of the short but agile forepaws against the rear of each pouch. The kangaroo rat withstands the desert's aridity by spending the hot daylight hours in the moist chambers of its elabo-rate burrow system and by conserving all available water: some is produced metabolically, even from dry seeds; some is absorbed for reuse from the gastrointestinal tract and bladder. To remove the excess oil and dirt from its fur, the kangaroo rat need have only sand in which to take a dust bath. A clean animal, it also has a gentle temperament, except when faced with others of its kind.

      Really a biped, the kangaroo rat travels by hopping on its long hind feet, making an audible thud at each landing. When it is moving rapidly, its tail streams out behind, a useful rudder for maneuvering quick and devious turns to elude predators. Look, therefore, for a trail showing only hind feet and the tip of a tail. Very acute hearing is another defense. The kangaroo rat can detect an owl in flight or a rattlesnake coiling to strike. The female of the species usually bears six young a year—three in the spring and three in the fall, the periods of new vegetation growth.

The larger Great Basin kangaroo rat *(D. microps),* also called the chisel-toothed kangaroo rat, lives in the hot desert valleys of southeast Oregon and southern Idaho. On its tail the dark stripes are wider than the light ones. One of its common names derives from the chisel shape of the lower incisors. Those of the other species are pointed. Reportedly these "chisels" enable the Great Basin kangaroo

HEERMANN KANGAROO RAT *(Dipodomys heermanni)*

NORTHERN GRASSHOPPER MOUSE *(Onychomys leucogaster)*

rat to scrape off and get beneath the salty skin of its preferred foods, which are members of the goosefoot family (chenopods), such as winter fat. This kangaroo rat, therefore, prefers areas principally vegetated by chenopods; the Ord kangaroo rat chooses a more mixed vegetation. The very dark foot-long (305 mm) Heermann kangaroo rat *(D. heermanni)* crosses the border from California into southwestern Oregon. Its distinguishing mark is a white-tipped tail.

Northern grasshopper mouse *(Onychomys leucogaster)*
The northern grasshopper mouse measures only 5¼ to 5½ inches (133 to 140 mm) because its short tail is less than half the length of its head and body. It is a stocky little animal, with the pointed nose and long ears of a deer mouse. Its coat is a light grayish brown above, white beneath.

The northern grasshopper mouse roams through the sage

SAGEBRUSH VOLE *(Lagurus curtatus)*

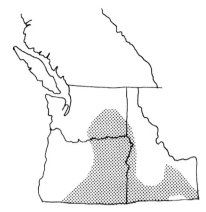

Onychomys leucogaster

and greasewood of the Great Basin and the Columbia Basin. It is a mighty mouse for its size, an efficient little hunter which tracks down grasshoppers, crickets, and other insects for 80 percent of its diet, but also regularly kills other types of mice equal to itself in size. This little nocturnal predator has been likened to a weasel—never common, ranging over a relatively large territory, fearless in the hunt, occupying the burrows of its prey or of other larger animals. It has strong claws effective in capturing and holding until it can bite the back of its victim's neck with its lower incisors. I have seen grasshopper mice in the lab dealing with such nasty customers as scorpions and darkling beetles. The proper techniques are not instinctive, for the youngsters were sprayed in the face time and again by the beetles until, by trial and error, they learned to push the bugs' abdomens down in the sand and start feeding on the heads.

One zoologist who had a captive grasshopper mouse for about three years reported that it was friendly to others of its kind but relished all meat, delighted to gnaw on chop bones. Given the freedom of the kitchen at night, it would clean out all the cockroaches that were not inaccessibly ensconced on the upper shelves (it is no climber). He also confirmed that the grasshopper mouse does indeed howl like a tiny wolf, usually in the spring. Several other of its sounds have been recorded. The grasshopper mouse is active all winter and most certainly is a friend to man for its aid in keeping down insect populations.

Sagebrush vole *(Lagurus curtatus)*
The sagebrush vole is a small, light gray mouse, four to five inches (102 to 127 mm), with a very short tail, as well as the blunt nose and small ears characteristic of voles.

The sagebrush vole lives amid the bunchgrass and the scat-

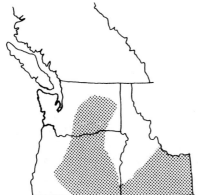

Lagurus curtatus

tered sagebrush scrub of the Arid Transition and Upper Sonoran life zones. Look for it mainly in the upland areas, however, from an elevation of about 2,000 feet (610 m) and up. Though its habitat is different, its habits are quite typically volelike. Active during the day, this vole makes runways that are poorly formed on the dry ground and are frequently marked by piles of feces. It will eat nearly anything green, and plants are its source of water as well as of food. Having once engaged in the delightful task of examining mouse stomach contents, I can vouch for the fact that this vole is also a flower eater. One researcher in Oregon has written up the sagebrush vole's use of cow chips, which it can hollow out for food and also use as shelter. The burrows of this vole are often arranged in colonies, presumably family groupings. The nests within the burrows are made of sagebrush bark or grass stems. Here young sagebrush voles are born at any season of the year.

ALSO LOOK FOR: Merriam shrew
White-tailed jackrabbit
Nuttall cottontail
Townsend and other ground squirrels
Desert wood rat

Arid Cliff and Rocky Outcrop

As with the moister rocky areas of the high mountains, the arid cliffs and rocky outcrops form a habitat attracting several species for the safety it can provide. Again, this is a "bed and board" situation: the animals choosing to shelter among the rocks will range abroad, to a greater or lesser degree, into the surrounding type of vegetation. This association belongs to no single life zone, but usually rises out of the sagebrush desert or the dry grasslands. It shares their burning, dry summers and cool winters. Its main representation is the basaltic outcroppings and rimrocks of the Columbia and Great basins. Juniper, sage, and mountain mahogany grow in its vicinity.

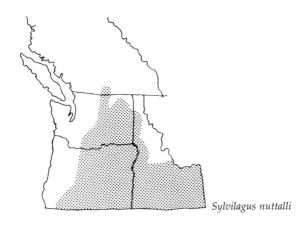

Sylvilagus nuttalli

Nuttall cottontail, mountain cottontail *(Sylvilagus nuttalli)*
The Nuttall is a rabbit, about 13½ inches (343 mm) long, with a tail that looks like a white powder puff—as a good cottontail's should. Its general body color is not unlike that of the other native rabbits, a grayish brown, but with a definite gray emphasis.

This rabbit lives amid the rocky outcrops and brushy thickets of the sagebrush country, but does spread from the Upper Sonoran into the dry, treeless portion of the Transition Life Zone. It is not a particularly swift runner nor one that employs the evasive zigzags of the jackrabbits. Instead it goes straight for the protective cover of rocks or thick brush when alarmed. Occasionally it tries a freezing tactic. Like

NUTTALL COTTONTAIL *(Sylvilagus nuttalli)*

YELLOW-BELLIED MARMOT *(Marmota flaviventris)*

other rabbits, it is probably most active in the very early morning and from sundown into the twilight hours. Sometimes it may even be seen feeding at midday. It makes narrow foraging trails throughout the brush and feeds on sage, local grasses, and succulent plants. These must provide water as well as food. Fur-lined nests fill cup-shaped depressions that lie about six inches (15 cm) deep in the ground. During the spring and summer several litters of blind, helpless young, about four to six per litter, are born in these nests.

Yellow-bellied marmot *(Marmota flaviventris)*
Marmots look like very large, overfed squirrels. This particular species is some twenty-three to twenty-four inches (584 to 610 mm) long. Its

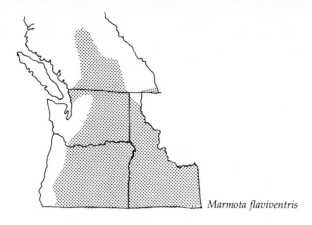
Marmota flaviventris

coat is grizzled on the back but distinctly yellow on the underparts.

In the Pacific Northwest this marmot is generally associated with the basaltic outcrops of the eastern regions. It also takes to abandoned buildings, piles of logs or lumber, and the roadside banks provided by man. In the Rocky Mountains it ascends to the alpine meadows, territory that in the Cascades is occupied instead by the hoary marmot.

The marmots are diurnal plant foragers, heavy-bodied and not overly fast-moving, and thus quite vulnerable to predation. They usually maintain special rocks as lookout posts "manned" by sentinels. A short, sharp warning whistle sends the rest of the colony rushing for homes deep in the rock crevices. In the spring the marmots may also be seen stretched out atop the rocks just sunning themselves. In the hot lowlands the yellow-bellied marmot goes into a dormant state in late June or July and passes right from this period of aestivation into one of hibernation for the duration of the cold winter months. It reappears between February and April, depending upon elevation. Breeding occurs soon after emergence and an average of five young are born two months later upon a bed of dry grass within the safety of the marmot's rocky den.

Canyon mouse *(Peromyscus crinitus)*
The canyon mouse is small but has a long tail, giving it a total of about seven inches (178 mm). It has rather long and silky fur which is yellowish buff above and whitish below on both body and tail.

The canyon mouse lives in arid rocky canyons, basaltic outcroppings, and rimrock. In this inhospitable environment it makes its home in a hole or a crack in the cliffs, coming out only after dark. It lives mainly on seeds; the shells and husks may be found scattered along the

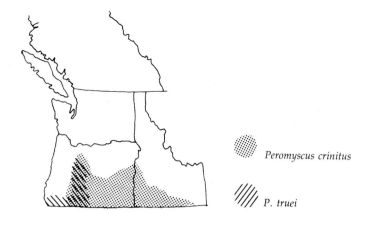

Peromyscus crinitus

P. truei

rocky ledges outside its dwelling. Seeds provide the canyon mouse with water. Its only other source is whatever little moisture may be lapped up from the sides of rocks. There is some evidence to suggest that during the driest time of the year this mouse may restrict its activity and reduce its metabolic rate and evaporative water loss by entering a state of shallow torpor.

Only slightly larger than the canyon mouse, the piñon mouse (*P. truei*) is more like the deer mouse in coloration—brown above and white underneath. It can be distinguished from all other *Peromyscus*, however, by its large ears, measuring one inch (25 mm) or longer. Its name derives from its characteristic habitat of piñon pine and juniper woodlands in California. In southern and central Oregon it can be found associated with basaltic cliffs, canyon walls, and dry brushy areas of the Upper Sonoran Life Zone. Again like the deer mouse, the piñon mouse is nocturnal, is partial to a very varied diet, and is known to enter cabins and other isolated structures.

Bushy-tailed wood rat (*Neotoma cinerea*)
Ratlike in its size (some fifteen to sixteen inches, 381 to 406 mm), the bushy-tailed wood rat rather resembles an overgrown deer mouse with its large eyes and ears and its coloration. The adult coat is grayish brown dorsally and white ventrally; that of the juvenile, more blue gray on the back. This wood rat has a lovely bushy tail and long whiskers.

The bushy-tailed wood rat inhabits cliffs, broken rock, and talus at almost any elevation. It is also notorious for taking up residence in abandoned mines or old cabins, leaving its typical musky odor and piles of half-inch-long dark fecal pellets as telltale evidence. Its natural home is the rock cave and the crevice, even the ledge, but rarely the

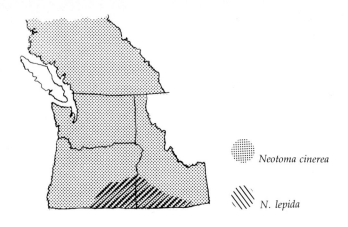

 *Neotoma cinerea*

N. lepida

large stick pile construction for which the dusky-footed wood rat is known. White incrustations on the rocks are signs of habitation by many generations of wood rats that have urinated there. The home of the "pack rat" (as all wood rats are sometimes called) is decorated by its booty, and anything it is able to transport is fair "game." Shiny metallic items are especially prized. One wood rat dwelling on Mount Rainier yielded the following: nest—rags, leaves, paper, glove thumb, string, thongs, oakum; food stores—apple core, onion peel, bacon rind, raisins, chocolate bars, figs, puffballs, bread crust, meat scraps, cantaloupe rind, potatoes, dried apricots, lemons, mushrooms, beans, peanuts, banana, lumps of sugar; miscellaneous—dime, coffee can lid, paraffin, bones, pieces of candle, and several cakes of soap.

Wood rats are mostly herbivorous. They lay up some dried

BUSHY-TAILED WOOD RAT *(Neotoma cinerea)*

plants for winter use, although they remain nocturnally active throughout the year. Despite their agility at running, climbing, and jumping, they have many enemies, including foxes, coyotes, owls, and large snakes. Wood rats communicate seldom by voice, but not infrequently by a drumming of the hind feet. A litter of three or four young is born in the spring and sometimes again later in the year.

The desert wood rat (*N. lepida*) is about a foot (305 mm) long and has a round tail. It likes the rocky areas of the Upper Sonoran Life Zone, as well as the desert scrub. It lives in rocks, clay banks, or burrows with shrub and cactus-shielded entrances and is seemingly able to negotiate cactus spines with impunity.

ALSO LOOK FOR: California and other ground squirrels
                Porcupine

FURTHER READING

The titles listed are works I have used as references, as well as other books dealing with one or more of the little mammals of the Pacific Northwest. For journal articles and scientific monographs, the reader is referred to bibliographies in the titles mentioned below, as for example, in Banfield or Hanney.

Bailey, Vernon. *The Mammals and Life Zones of Oregon.* U.S. Department of Agriculture, U.S. Bureau of Biological Survey, North American Fauna No. 55. Washington, D.C.: 1936. One of the older definitive works on the subspecies of a state, with a fuller exposition of habits and economic status than usual. Also includes a discussion of Oregon life zones, their climate, flora, and fauna.

Banfield, Alexander W. F. *The Mammals of Canada.* Toronto: University of Toronto Press, 1974. A comprehensive treatment of Canadian species, with one or more references provided for each. Thoroughly understandable to the layman, with illustrations in both color and black and white.

Barkalow, Frederick S. Jr., and Shorten, Monica. *The World of the Gray Squirrel.* Living World Books. Philadelphia: J. B. Lippincott, 1973. Although specifically concerned with the eastern gray squirrel, this book has good general information pertinent to the life histories and behavior of other tree squirrels.

Burt, William H., and Grossenheider, Richard P. *A Field Guide to the Mammals: Field Marks of All North American Species Found North of Mexico,* 3d ed. Peterson Field Guide Series. Boston: Houghton Mifflin, 1976. Contains some description of habits, habitat, and young, but primarily concerned with field recognition characters, illustrated in color. Also depicts North American distributions.

Cahalane, Victor H. *Mammals of North America.* New York: MacMillan, 1947. Poorly illustrated but offers a lot of information, including origins of names, pertinent Indian legends, and other stories.

Costello, David F. *The World of the Porcupine.* Living World Books. Philadelphia: J. B. Lippincott, 1966. Like the other "Living World Books," a good popular account of its subject animal, with several pages of references and a number of black-and-white photographs.

Cowan, Ian McTaggart, and Guiguet, Charles J. *The Mammals of British Columbia,* 3d rev. ed. Handbook No. 11. Victoria, B.C.: British Columbia Provincial Museum, 1965. A useful paperback with full treatment of subspecies for the province, including range maps. Species are illustrated in black and white.

Crowcroft, Peter. *The Life of the Shrew.* London: Max Reinhardt, 1957. Although based mainly on the European shrew, this is a worthwhile little book, not too scientific to be of interest to all.

Dalquest,Walter W. *Mammals of Washington.* University of Kansas Publications, Museum of Natural History, vol. 2. Lawrence, Kansas: University of Kansas, 1948. A classic reference for Washington State's mammals, giving full descriptions and details of distribution at the subspecies level.

Davis, William B. *The Recent Mammals of Idaho.* Contribution from Museum of Vertebrate Zoology, University of California, Berkeley. Caldwell, Idaho: Caxton Printers, 1939. Another in the category of the classic state references. Covers details of Idaho subspecies and their records of occurrence.

Gunderson, Harvey L. *Mammalogy.* New York: McGraw-Hill, 1976. A textbook, the chapters of which include a review of the Mammalia by family, a history of mammalogy in the United States, and a reasonably long bibliography.

Hall, Eugene R., and Kelson, Keith R. *The Mammals of North America,* 2 vols., New York: Ronald Press, 1959. An essential reference work for the mammalogist. Gives identification, classification, and range of the mammals of this continent, including keys to the species and skull drawings.

Hanney, Peter W. *Rodents: Their Lives and Habits.* New York: Tapplinger Publishing, 1975. Attempts a general picture, including reasons for success, of the different rodent groups—climbers, burrowers, etc. Complete with index, references, black-and-white photographs, and drawings.

Henisch, Bridget A., and Henisch, Heinz K. *Chipmunk Portrait.* State College, Pennsylvania: Carnation Press, 1970. A slight but entertaining introduction to chipmunk natural history, as well as to the chipmunk in art, literature, and history. Lavishly illustrated in black and white.

Ingles, Lloyd G. *Mammals of the Pacific States: California, Oregon, and Washington.* Stanford: Stanford University Press, 1965. Excellent field guide; also provides additional data on many mammals. A series of useful appendices include a selected bibliography, illustrations of scats, and methods for collecting and preparing study specimens.

Larrison, Earl J. *Mammals of the Northwest: Washington, Oregon, Idaho and British Columbia.* The Trailside Series. Seattle: Seattle Audubon Society, 1976. An extensive revision of an earlier work. Has a good format, with identifying characters and range of species separated from the rest of the text.

MacClintock, Dorcas. *Squirrels of North America.* New York: Van Nostrand Reinhold, 1970. A readable review of the family Sciuridae, with quotes from other authors scattered through the substantial sections on habits. Includes range maps, drawings, and lists of references.

Merriam, Clinton H. "The Geographic Distribution of Life in North America: With Special Reference to the Mammalia." *Smithsonian Institution Annual Report to July, 1891,* pp. 365-415. Washington, D.C.: 1893.

Rue, Leonard Lee III. *Pictorial Guide to the Mammals of North America.* New York: Thomas Crowell, 1967. A listing of vital statistics, plus more extensive information on common species. Good black-and-white photographs, range maps, and examples of tracks.

—*The World of the Beaver.* Living World Books. Philadelphia: J. B. Lippincott, 1964. The beaver's life through the seasons of the year and its relations with man. Many black-and-white photographs.

Schaefer, Jack W. *An American Bestiary.* Boston: Houghton Mifflin, 1975. This New Mexico author provides a more literary and historical view than usual of shrews, lagomorphs, pocket gophers, porcupines, and the members of the pocket mouse-kangaroo rat family.

Schoonmaker, Walter J. *The World of the Woodchuck.* Living World Books. Philadelphia: J. B. Lippincott, 1966. A good popular account which, like the other volumes in this series, traces the life history of a particular animal through spring, summer, autumn, and winter.

Taylor, Walter P., and Shaw, William T. *Mammals and Birds of Mount Rainier National Park.* U.S. Department of Interior, National Park Service. Washington, D.C.: 1927. Interesting accounts and local occurrences with photographs by such distinguished naturalists of the time as William Finley.

INDEX

Boldface numerals refer to pages on which black-and-white photographs are located.

OTHER PAPERBACKS
FROM PACIFIC SEARCH PRESS

Cooking

Bone Appétit! Natural Foods for Pets by Frances Sheridan Goulart. Treat your pet to some home-cooked meals made only with pure, natural ingredients. Recipes fit for both man and beast! Drawings. 96 pp. $2.95.

The Carrot Cookbook by Ann Saling. Over 200 mouth-watering recipes. 160 pp. $3.50.

The Dogfish Cookbook by Russ Mohney. Over 65 piscine delights. Cartoons and drawings. 108 pp. $1.95.

The Green Tomato Cookbook by Paula Simmons. More than 80 solutions to the bumper crop. 96 pp. $2.95.

Why Wild Edibles? The Joys of Finding, Fixing, and Tasting—West of the Rockies by Russ Mohney. Color and black-and-white photos plus illustrations. 320 pp. $6.95.

Wild Mushroom Recipes by the Puget Sound Mycological Society. 2d edition. Over 200 recipes. 178 pp. $6.95.

The Zucchini Cookbook by Paula Simmons. Revised and enlaroed 2d edition. Over 150 tasty creations. 160 pp. $3.50.

Nature

Butterflies Afield in the Pacific Northwest by William Neill/Douglas Hepburn, photography. Lovely guide with 74 unusual color photos of living butterflies. 96 pp. $5.95.

Cascade Companion by Susan Schwartz/Bob and Ira Spring, photography. Nature and history of the Washington Cascades. Black-and-white photos, maps. 160 pp. $5.95.

Common Seaweeds of the Pacific Coast by J. Robert Waaland. Introduction to the world of the seaweed—its biology, conservation, and many uses to both industry and seafood lovers. Color and black-and-white photos. 136 pp. $5.95.

Fire and Ice: The Cascade Volcanoes by Stephen L. Harris. Copublished with The Mountaineers. Black-and-white photos and drawings, maps. 320 pp. $7.50.

Living Shores of the Pacific Northwest by Lynwood Smith/Bernard Nist, photography. Fascinating guide to seashore life. Over 140 photos, 110 in color. 160 pp. $9.95.

Minnie Rose Lovgreen's Recipe for Raising Chickens by Minnie Rose Lovgreen. 2d edition, 32 pp. $2.00.

Sleek & Savage: North America's Weasel Family by Delphine Haley. Extraordinary color and black-and-white photos; bibliography. 128 pp. $5.50.

Toothed Whales: In Eastern North Pacific and Arctic Waters compiled by Alice Seed. 2d edition. 40 pp. $1.75.